RUMI'S DIVAN OF SHEMS OF TABRIZ

James Cowan is the author of numerous books on Tribalism and Aboriginal spirituality. His journeys to remote parts of the world in order to hear the voice of tribal people are central to his work. In recent years, he has written poetry, fiction, children's stories and philosophic essays. His work, *A Mapmaker's Dream*, a work of fiction, explores the subjectivity of old maps. At present he lives among the Kukatja people in the Tanami Desert, NW Australia, where he supervises their art programme.

Element Classics of World Spirituality

The writings and teachings of the great spiritual masters are brought together in the *Element Classics of World Spirituality* series. These volumes focus on the philosophical and religious meaning of the texts and their abiding relevance. They are introduced by internationally recognized scholars and spiritual leaders, who highlight and enhance the richness and depth of the writings.

In the same series

The Bhagavad Gita
The Cloud of Unknowing
The Dhammapada
The Pilgrim's Progress
The Tao Te Ching

ELEMENT CLASSICS OF
WORLD SPIRITUALITY

Rumi's Divan of Shems of Tabriz

Selected Odes

MEVLANA JALÁLUDDIN RUMI

A New Interpretation by James Cowan

ELEMENT

Rockport, Massachusetts ● Shaftesbury, Dorset
Brisbane, Queensland

© Element Books Limited 1997
Text © James Cowan 1992

First published in Great Britain in 1995
as *Where Two Oceans Meet* by
Element Books Limited
Shaftesbury, Dorset

This edition first published in the USA in 1997 by
Element, Inc.
PO Box 830, Rockport, MA 01966

Published in Great Britain in 1997 by
Element Books Limited
Shaftesbury, Dorset

Published in Australia in 1997 by
Element Books Limited
for Jacaranda Wiley Limited
33 Park Road, Milton, Brisbane 4064

Cover design by Bridgewater Book Company
Page design by Linda Reed and Joss Nizan
Typeset by Footnote Graphics, Warminster, Wilts
Printed and bound in the USA by
Courier Westford Inc., Westford, MA

British Library Cataloguing in Publication
data available

Library of Congress Cataloging in Publication
data available

ISBN 1-85230-919-9

Contents

Introduction

1

Your love has made me drunk, my hands are trembling.
I am intoxicated. I don't know what I'm doing.

Mevlana Jaláluddin Rumi

Hearing these words echo in my thoughts that evening
as the bus entered the winter-deserted streets of Konya in
central Turkey, I somehow knew how Mevlana Jaláluddin
Rumi must have felt. My hands too were trembling, indeed
sweating a little, in spite of the snow scattering like
disturbed butterflies before our headlamps. Two elderly
peasant women lounging in the seats opposite peeled
apples and carefully ate everything, including cores and
seeds. Across their laps a child slept, oblivious to the feast.
They had travelled like this all the way from Istanbul, their
mutual silence redolent with the aroma of new apples.

So divine and unabashed, Rumi's words of apparent
confusion continued to run through my mind as we
headed towards the bus terminal. They represented the
beginning of my own encounter with one of the true
masters of Persian poetry, a man who had made his love of
another the cornerstone of his quest for union with God.

I don't know why I felt the need to visit Rumi's tomb in
Central Anatolia. After all, he had died over 700 years ago,
and his remains would be no more than dust. Yet there was
some quality about his personality which drew me into the
remote steppes of what had once been the heartland of the
Seljuk Empire. Like him, perhaps, I was drawn by the
prospect of gazing upon the minarets of this ancient
capital, a city renowned as a spiritual centre long before he
had ever settled here. The entire region had once witnessed

a confluence of peoples, ideas and religions much as Jerusalem had done before it. Christian had lived alongside Moslem; Crusader alongside Saracen; Turk alongside Arab, Jew, and Byzantine. For Konya had been the hub of a wheel whose axle extended far beyond this rutted Land of Rum,[1] scene of so many wars and conflicts over the centuries. It was a city dedicated to the spirit – a city ripe for the nurturing of a young man into a poet, and a poet into one who to this day is looked upon as the most savoured fruit of Islam.

Mevlana Jaláluddin Rumi, the greatest mystic poet of his age, was born at Balkh in the northern province of Khorasan in AD 1207. He came from a family of jurists and scholars. His father, Bahauddin Muhammed ibn al-Husain al-Khatibi al-Baqri (1148–1231), was a man of considerable learning, who bore the title 'King of Scholars' (*Sultan-ul-'Ulema*). However, Rumi's scholarly father grew up in an era hostile to metaphysical inquiry. This had been provoked by an attack on philosophy by many contemporary theologians under the spell of Aristotelian thought, led by such men as Ibn Sina (Avicenna). The noted philosopher al-Ghazali (died AD 1111), who himself underwent a spiritual crisis late in his life which forced him to explore the practices of Sufism more deeply than hitherto, successfully attacked these rationalists, earning for himself the title 'Argument of Islam' (*Hujjat-ul-Islam*) in the process.

Such was the influence of the rationalists, however, that Rumi's father found it difficult to teach with impunity. Though the Shah of Khorasan admired his gifts, on one occasion sending him the keys to his treasury as a mark of respect, he soon found himself maligned by one of the Shah's own courtiers, the rationalist philosopher Fakhruddin Razi. The relationship between Bahauddin and Razi became so strained that the former decided to quit the kingdom with his family and journey to Nishapur. His decision to leave may also have been influenced by the Mongol invasions under the leadership of Khengiz Khan, which were already devastating much of the region. Political instability, combined with intellectual harassment, finally forced Bahauddin to seek another haven for his family in 1213.

Rumi would have been a boy of about five at this time. The great teacher and celebrated poet, Ferideddin Attar, welcomed their caravan to Nishapur in the hope that Bahauddin might be persuaded to stay and teach in the home of his forefathers. But it seems that Rumi's father was intent on making the pilgrimage to Baghdad and Mecca, an obligation for all Moslems at some time in their lives. It appears that Attar was deeply impressed by the young Rumi while he was in Nishapur and made a gift to the boy of his own work, the 'Book of the Mysteries' (Esrarname). It is said that Attar, watching Rumi depart a few steps behind his father on the road to Baghdad, remarked to one of those with him: 'What an astonishing sight! There goes a river dragging a mighty ocean behind it.' Here was the first intimation of Rumi's unfathomable effect on all those who met him. Clearly that quality of baraka (grace) already permeated his being.

There followed a period of wandering which lasted 16 years, before the party finally reached Konya. During this time the family visited Baghdad, Mecca, Medina, Jerusalem, Damascus, Arzinjin and Larinda. These were the sites traditionally visited by learned Moslems, and so formed the mandatory pilgrimage for any scholar such as Bahauddin. Meanwhile, at eighteen, Rumi married his childhood friend Gevher Hatun, the daughter of one of his father's closest friends, whose family had accompanied them on their journey. Soon after, his first two sons, Sultan Veled and Aladdin Chelebi, were born. Throughout these years Rumi continued to sit at the feet of his father and his followers, learning everything possible about the mysteries of the Islamic faith. His contact with wise philosophers in all the great capitals of the region further deepened his understanding. The family reached Konya in 1229, and on the death of his father two years later Rumi was ready to receive the mantle of 'King of Scholars'.

The hagiography surrounding Rumi's early life and education amply serves to reinforce the idea that he was 'touched by God'. During the next ten years he dedicated himself to intensive study under one of his father's close friends, Burhanuddin. He travelled back and forth to Damascus and Aleppo, two important centres of learning in the thirteenth century. Here he met with such men as Kamaluddin who taught him all they knew. It was only after he had completed a course of mortification and ascetic practices lasting 120 days, under the guidance of Burhanuddin, that his master believed the younger man had attained to absolute purity. Burhanuddin remarked to him: 'You were unparalleled in the realm of rational, traditional, spiritual and acquisitive knowledge. Now at this moment you find yourself unsurpassed in the knowledge of divine secrets.' At 34, Mevlana Jaláluddin Rumi found himself a spiritual leader among men, a *khalifah* or vice-regent of God on earth.

One would assume at this point that Rumi was the ideal embodiment of the young spiritual. Learned beyond his years, blessed with family connections that linked him to many of the *ulema* of the Middle East, already the head of a flourishing ascetic community and small *medrese* (religious school) in Konya, his future as a teacher and philosopher seemed assured. His reputation already extended well beyond the boundaries of the Seljuk Empire, and men such as Muhyiddin ibn Arabi (1165–1240), Islam's foremost mystical philosopher, occasionally met for discussions with him. The purity of his belief and the elegance of his mystical insight struck a chord with many who longed to see the resurgence of Sufism throughout the Islamic world. In a sense, Rumi was looked upon as an icon by those who wished to encourage the final destruction of the rationalist element within Islam. Instead of dogma, people wanted mysteries; instead of academic dissertation, they wanted the soul's ascent towards Godhead to be made the central tenet of belief. *Hal*, the divine love or consciousness of God, became Rumi's password into his heightened state of awareness.

Rumi's life until this point had followed a well-trodden path towards mystical insight. He conformed to certain archetypes. Recognized at an early age by accepted wise men of his time, well travelled in the tradition of pilgrim and sage, well married with a growing family among his responsibilities, he might have looked forward to a conventional life as scholar and teacher. According to those who knew him well, it was a life that suited him. Heir to his father's legacy, all he had to do from then on was teach, write, and meet with learned men – and so uphold the time-honoured tradition of a Sufi wise man and saint. Such a life was his destiny, it appeared, until that fateful day when he met Shems-i-Tabriz for the first time.

2

Nick-named *Parindah*, meaning 'the flier', Shems was an old man of around 60 when he first encountered Rumi. He had been born into the Assassin tribe[2] of Hasan B Sabbah, of which his grandfather, Nuruddin Muhammad, had for a time been chief. His Sufi teacher, Ebubekir, had been a basket-weaver in Tabriz. Long before he joined a Sufi order, however, legend has it that Shems had always been unusual, a boy gifted with a sharp, unconventional mind who rarely saw things as they appeared. A story tells of how, when his father took him to the edge of a stream, they saw a hen which had hatched a clutch of ducklings, cackling with alarm. The ducklings had dived into the stream and were swimming about, much to the confusion of their adopted mother. Shems then turned to his father and said: 'Father, look at them! They're just like you and me. While the hen is clucking anxiously on the bank, her young ones have dived into the stream and swum to the other side. Now you can see the difference between inherent and acquired characteristics, can't you?' If this story is true, then Shems already knew that his destiny was to champion that which was inherent in a man's soul, rather than what might be acquired by way of rational investigation.

This does not mean that Shems' journey towards knowledge of *hal* was made any easier. His eccentric behaviour and his inability to suffer fools readily made him a target for disdain and ridicule. Like Rumi, he journeyed throughout Persia and Arabia in search of suitable teachers. He despised anyone who proclaimed mystical insight as their own, or mouthed pious epithets instead of expressing basic knowledge. When one sheikh (a Moslem spiritual authority) asked him why he had come to him, Shems replied that he was 'searching for knowledge of God'. To this the sheikh answered, 'God rules in the heavens and moves the ships in their course.' Disgusted by such an expression of facile piety, Shems stood up and left without saying another word.

He was also wary of those who insisted that the bond between themselves and their sheikh automatically bound them to knowledge of truth. He hated spiritual elitism. As far as he was concerned, the Prophet of God himself (Muhammed) had placed the mantle on his shoulders in the spiritual world. This cloak was not one to wear thin in two days, or to rot and tear before being tossed aside. According to Shems, the cloak was that of truth, and existed 'beyond time and place, yesterday, today or tomorrow'. What, after all, has love to do with time and place?

Furthermore, he insisted that truth could not be reached with words or even science, but only by divine union, by obedience to canon law, by learning from a mature teacher and guide, and by experiencing love and affection. These, not the dialectical gymnastics of the philosophers, were the hallmarks of true understanding. 'In philosophy, there are ten forms of reasoning which claim to cover the universe. Yet when none of these leads to truth, the philosopher scratches his head, still refusing to learn from his failure.' Accordingly Shems claimed that divine knowledge, which is above all knowledge, cannot be learned through excessive study. No knowledge can compare with the enlightenment obtained by union with God. The 'wisdom of the heart' was for him the only real source of truth. In the West such knowledge was described by Thomas Aquinas (1225–74) as 'connatural' – that is, knowledge of a kind which is produced in the intellect, but not by virtue of conceptual connections or by way of demonstration.

Shems further maintained that everything is sacrificed to man, while man is sacrificed only to himself, to his own inherent truth. Although God said that he exalted man, he did not command the exaltation of the sky or his own throne. Reaching the throne precludes any need to ascend higher. Likewise, it is useless to descend seven layers under the ground in the hope of finding him. Instead, all you have to do is *enter a man's heart* and there befriend him. Knowledge of the heart, and the heart only, is the key to enlightenment. When a man knows himself he knows all.

Shems also believed that slavery to God was slavery of the heart, and service to God was service of the heart. In this way a man can become immersed in ecstatic contemplation of God, the key to which is divine law. When the Prophet said: 'To think for one moment, to attain ecstasy and to bend to the heart, these are better than 60 years of worship', what he meant was that a loyal dervish (a man who is vowed to a life of poverty and spirituality) can only find peace in the heart. Turning towards God, and surrender to God, are acts of the heart.

Throughout his life Shems practised a form of madness or the cult of the fool. His feigned incoherence or apparent madness on occasion, whether as an expression of faith in unreason and in a topsy-turvy world, or as a device for concealing his beliefs, was closely related to a particular brand of Sufism derived from pre-Islamic Persian myths and beliefs. 'Acting the fool' was not uncommon among many dissident groups that found orthodoxy inimical to their desire to attain mystical union. Shems' background as a member of the Assassin sect, which was of Ismaeli rather than Sunni origin, would likely have brought him into contact with such groups.[3] Owing their allegiance to a shadowy figure known as the 'Old Man of the Mountain' (*Aloadin*), these people regularly practised mind-altering hallucinogenic methods using hashish (from which the word 'assassin' is derived). According to Marco Polo, the use of such drugs was designed to instil a belief in a 'beautiful garden running with conduits of wine and milk and honey and water, and full of lovely women for the delectation of all its inmates'. In other words, Paradise on earth!

Shems' Shi'ite origins would have made him amenable to the idea of the Hidden Imam, or God's appointed regent on earth, which is a central tenet of the Ismaeli faith. Searching for the Hidden Imam, the Divine Friend, became a part of his life. He used to go on long journeys seeking someone who was aware of the truth, a man of the heart. He would stay at inns and caravanserais along his route. If he were ever recognized, he would immediately make his escape, preferring the anonymity of some other inn where he could lock himself away for days on end, rather than deal with adoring pilgrims. There he would practise asceticism, living for many days on a jug of water and a loaf of bread. His object on these journeys was to find a sheikh who might lead him to more authentic levels of mystical insight. Always travelling, searching, questioning and examining those who claimed to be sheikhs, his restlessness took him to many parts of the Islamic world. As he said: 'I set out to find a sheikh from my own land, but all my troubles were for nothing. Everyone I met was empty, yet I still felt sure there must be one person, somewhere . . . that the world couldn't becompletely empty. But I never found him.' Above all, he was looking for a teacher, not disciples; a friend and guide, not a servant.

His distrust of falsely acquired mystical knowledge invariably led to arguments with various sheikhs whom he met. On one occasion he stopped in Baghdad and paid a visit to a well-known sheikh, Evhaduddin Mirmani. He found the man gazing into a bowl of water. When Shems asked him what he was doing, the sheikh replied: 'I am watching the moon in this basin.' In disgust, Shems retorted: 'If you don't have a boil on the back of your neck, lift up your head and look at the sky! There you will see the moon as it is, instead of in a basin. Why are you leaning over basins when all you are really doing is depriving yourself of what you are really looking for?' It was Shems' adherence to reality, to the world as it was, that marked him out as a radical at a time when Sufis were increasingly practising an overly refined form of asceticism.

At 60, Shems had still not found the guide he was looking for. His eccentric behaviour and continual wanderings set him apart from his contemporaries. Not wishing to found a school of his own and reluctant to embrace the traditional path of the dervish, he had in a sense grown wild, become an unbroken spirit who longed to encounter a spirit as free as his own. He represented a force, an energy, masculine and alive, which somehow had to be channelled into a new form of spirituality. In the company of scholars he became impatient with their penchant for learned dissertation; while in the company of Sufi dervishes he grew tired of their false mysticism and piety. There was nowhere for him to turn. He had travelled the world and met no one capable of matching their wits with his at that high level of genuine metaphysical inquiry to which he aspired.

3

Wrapped in a coarse black coat, Shems arrived in Konya in the late November of 1244 and took a room at an inn. A dream had urged him to make the journey in search of Mevlana Jaláluddin Rumi, whose reputation as a great teacher was already well known to him. Some reports suggest that Shems and Rumi had already met briefly, in Damascus, though these have never been confirmed. In any event, Shems knew that Rumi represented his last chance of meeting a man with the same spiritual rigour as himself.

The day after his arrival Shems awoke and went to sit in the paved courtyard in front of the inn so as to watch the people passing by. Towards the time of afternoon prayers a man approached, riding a mule, and followed by a number of students. It was Rumi, returning to his *medrese*. Shems looked at his short beard and tanned, wheat-coloured skin, and immediately liked what he saw.

Shems rose and approached the entourage. Without warning, he took hold of the mule's reins and abruptly asked a question of Rumi: 'Can you tell me, Mevlana Muhammed Jaláluddin, whether the Lord Mohammed or Beyazid-i Bestami is the greater man?'

Realizing that the question posed by this unknown man before him was likely to be a riddle, Rumi replied, 'Without doubt, the Lord Mohammed is the greater.'

Shems merely smiled. 'Did not the Lord Mohammed say: "God! I glorify You. We did not know Your worth." Whereas Bestami said, "I glorify myself. My reputation is great because there is no being but God in every part of my body." How do you explain this?'

Aware that the questioning might follow this course, Rumi responded at once: 'The Lord Mohammed spoke the way he did because each day he progressed many stages. Each time he reached a level of new understanding, he begged God's forgiveness for his previous lack of knowledge and errors. Only the Prophet has the endurance to contemplate God in abstraction, purified from all else, in all His manifestation, without remaining at any one stage of judgement. In contrast, Bestami was carried away by his arrival at the very first stage and, intoxicated by this attainment, went no further.'

Shems was deeply impressed by Rumi's statement and went down on his knees before the sage. Aware that this unknown dervish had deliberately tried to test him, Rumi climbed down from his mule and raised Shems to his feet. The two men gazed at one another, then embraced. As one chronicler related, it was as if two oceans had met. No word was exchanged between them as, arm in arm, Rumi and Shems walked home to the *medrese*. About them, students and townsfolk alike watched the incident with astonishment. No one could begin to understand what had passed between the two men since neither had apparently met the other before.

Rumi invited Shems to join him as a guest in his house. Inwardly he had already acknowledged that in Shems he had found a man whose spiritual attainment matched his own. Though nearly twice his age, Shems and he were nevertheless equals. It was left to Shems, however – the wayfarer and spiritual vagabond – to propose one more test for his new-found guide. He asked Rumi for a glass of wine, knowing that most dervishes regarded alcohol with horror. Without a word Rumi asked that wine be brought and placed before his friend.

'You are a man of far greater powers than I thought,' Shems said. 'As a man of perfection, there is no one in the world to equal you.'

Shems then poured the wine away and embraced Rumi. At that point their divine friendship was confirmed. In knowing one another they had chosen unity rather than division, and only death could ever separate them. Entering the heart of a friend was for these men the first step towards union with God himself. As Dante was to relate later in *La Vita Nuova*: 'Behold, a god more powerful than I comes to rule over me.' Shems and Rumi knew they had embarked upon a journey of discovery whose object was divine union itself.[4] It appeared that a god more powerful than either of them had at last come home to roost in their souls.

What occurred between Rumi and Shems in the ensuing months was to bring an entirely new spiritual dimension to Islamic mysticism. The two friends locked themselves away for days at a time in *sobhet*, or mystical communion. What passed between them during these meetings has never been recorded in detail, but we do know that Shems spoke to Rumi of the love of God, and also that he introduced Rumi to the *sema*, a mystical dance that he had likely learnt through his Assassin affiliations. Each movement of the dance was laden with symbolic meaning: the slow turning of the body was likened to seeing God from all sides, and being enlightened by every aspect of Him; stamping the feet represented the crushing of the dancer's carnal nature underfoot; opening the arms reflected the way of perfection; and finally, prostration symbolised man's humility before God.

Shems took Rumi along the path he knew so well – that of divine love and ecstasy. In effect, the traveller must put all his trust in him who shows the way, and obediently follow in his footsteps. On such a journey occasions would arise when the lover and the beloved would become indistinguishable. Divine inspiration would be mutual and their love expressed in symbols. This divine love and ecstasy, this absolute devotion to God, inspired Shems and Rumi to a state of rapture as they danced the *sema* together. They had entered into the symbols, become wild with love – for God, through one another – and had thus partaken of divine union. Whirling together around the room, the two men were able to experience the eternal joy of rapture and mortality at one and the same time. The *sema* was the sweet food (ambrosia) of God's lovers, whereby they might taste the pleasure of this union and so be released from the tyranny of time and place.

To the sound of the *rebap* and *ney* (violin and flute), Shems spoke of friendship and divine love. On one occasion he informed Rumi: 'A true friend must be as mysterious as God. He must tolerate his friend's ugliness and faults, and not be offended by his mistakes. He must not turn away from him nor accuse him. Just as God's compassion leads him to forgive His subjects for their failings, He sustains them with an all-embracing kindness and compassion. This is the nature of unprejudiced and impartial friendship.'

For his part, Rumi was deeply affected by Shems' teachings. He had never met a person who so easily dismissed acquired knowledge in his pursuit of union. Shems was a man of passion, who relied on his deep intuition and feeling for reality to guide him on his spiritual journey. This was a new experience for Rumi who had never before encountered such a raw, unbridled approach to spirituality. When Shems threw all Rumi's books into the fountain one day, Rumi knew that to draw them out would be to admit defeat; to admit that his world – the world of books, well-turned aphorisms, learned dissertation, and the security of written knowledge – meant more to him than the reality of truth itself.

Shems was asking him to run naked into the wellsprings of *hal*, of divine love, and hope to drown rather than cling to what he already knew. His friend was demanding that Rumi make the ultimate sacrifice and join him on the adventure of a lifetime. Shems wanted Rumi to become a 'fool for God', a supreme dancer, a spiritual vagabond in the truest sense. No wonder Rumi became intoxicated while in Shems' company. As he later wrote: 'I was unripe and I have ripened. The sour expression on my face has gone at last. People say it shouldn't be like this, and neither do I since he [Shems] arrived and changed me.' Rumi further acknowledged: 'I was weak, I was an ascetic, yet I stood like a mountain, my legs firm in his presence. But no mountain is so strong that the memory of you [Shems] would not sweep it up like a wisp of straw and carry it away.'

Such was the charisma of their encounter that it was bound to affect Rumi's household. In the ensuing weeks he all but abandoned his public life as a teacher, neglected his family, and plunged ever deeper into his relationship with Shems. He poured praise upon Shems who, in turn, acknowledged Rumi as his spiritual master, saying: 'Thousands of Shems-i-Tabriz would be no more than a mote of dust in the vast tower of his greatness.' Inevitably their mutual love and respect aroused jealousies among Rumi's followers, who could see their master slipping away from them under the influence of this wild ascetic from Tabriz.

After an argument between Shems and one of Rumi's students, resentments were soon brought out in the open. Shems, who had openly 'pledged his head' for Rumi, was not about to suffer the petty jealousies of either students or townsfolk. The crisis point came when he and Rumi attended a ceremony together in Vizier Nusratuddin's *hanikah* (monastery). They sat in a corner of the hall, listening to scholars narrating the words of past seers they had read in books. After listening silently for some time, Shems was unable to contain himself any longer. He rose to his feet and announced: 'How much longer are you going to waste your time repeating the words of this or that scholar? When will you say, "My heart was inspired by

God"? Why are you walking with the staff of another? Where are your words and your works?'

By thus exposing the hypocrisy of the *ulema* of Konya Shems was left with little alternative but to leave the city, and in March 1246 he disappeared from Rumi's *medrese* without even advising his friend of where he was going. As he had arrived, so he departed: a lone traveller, a spiritual sojourner whose destination had been determined not by men but by God.

4

Deeply wounded by his friend's departure, Rumi retired to his cell and burned in the fire of bitterness at their separation. He found it impossible to understand why Shems should leave him when it was clear what they had meant to one another. Nothing would convince him that their love should be sundered like this. The only remedy he could find for his pain was to resort to a form of expression he had never attempted before: that of poetry. The scholar in him had been silenced, and from the ashes of this funeral pyre rose a new man fired with passion and the inflammatory nature of words. He began to write *ghazals* (short, rhyming, lyrical poems), calling upon his friend to return, pleading with him to understand his predicament.

> Know that with your departure my mind and faith have
> been stripped.
> This poor heart of mine no longer has patience or
> resolve.
>
> Don't ask me about my wan face, my troubled heart, or
> the burning in my soul.
> See with your own eyes, no power of words can explain
> these things.
>
> My face browns like a loaf baked in your heat,
> Now I crumble like stale bread, and am scattered.
>
> Like a mirror I reflect the images of your face, yet
> My own face, how it has grown pale, how wrinkled.

Poem after poem flowed from his pen, expressing his deep spiritual and emotional heartbreak. Nevertheless a new spirit of creativity had entered his soul. Mevlana Jaláluddin

Rumi was no longer the teacher, the scholar, the placid dervish whom people might approach for solace. Dominated by love, ecstasy and loss, he ascended to extreme heights of introspection in his attempts to come to terms with this newly acquired spirit moving within him. Shems' absence from his life forced him to reassess reality in the light of such spiritual intensity, drawn as it was from the deep well of his own consciousness. Could he survive such loneliness, or was he doomed to suffer grief for the rest of his life?

> Love came and the blood stopped flowing in my veins,
> Love washed over me and filled me with adoration.
>
> Every part of me was saturated with love, until
> Nothing remained but my name. All else was him.

Rumi was unable to dismiss the memory of Shems. He was possessed by his friend's dignity, his courage, and his willingness to go to any lengths in order to attain union with God. Such a man transcended all expectations previously demanded of the dervish. He was truly a wild being, whose very soul was in the grip of forces beyond those normally possessed by men. Shems represented the power of the angel, Zamyat, the eternal femininity of Earth, which lay beneath the surface of Ismaeli mysticism as a residue of earlier Persian belief. More importantly, he was a genuine *urafa*, a mystical gnostic, who had meditated tirelessly on truth to the point where he had been able to grasp the object, not in its objectivity, but as a sign, an intimation, that is ultimately the soul's annunciation of itself. In contrast, Rumi's loss was the loss of his soul's alter ego.

He wrote poems to Shems, calling upon him to return to Konya, wherever he might be. These were dispatched with messengers charged with the task of finding him. Rumi himself made the journey to Damascus in the hope of encountering his friend, but Shems was nowhere to be found. It seemed that he had disappeared from the face of the earth. Still Rumi pined for his *urafa*, the wild man from Tabriz, and longed for his return.

> I'm afraid to visit the places where you might be,
> Afraid of the jealousy of those who love you.
>
> Day and night you live in my heart,
> Gazing into my heart I see you there.

In another poem he wrote:

> Where are your precious words now?
> Where is that mind which solves all mysteries?
>
> Where is that foot walking in the rose-garden?
> The hand which held mine?

Finally Rumi received news that Shems had been seen in Damascus. He wrote at once, pleading for his friend to return to Konya, but his letter was ignored. More letters followed, none of which Shems deigned to answer. It was as if, by resisting Rumi's pleas, Shems was deliberately trying to push him to further extremes. He wanted Rumi to explore the very depths of longing before he might show himself again. But at last he announced his return to the bosom of the man whom he loved. Rumi replied at once:

> March O men, and bring me my beloved,
> Bring me him of unique excellence.

Sultan Veled, Rumi's son, was sent to Damascus to bring Shems back to Konya. He found the dervish in an inn playing chess. Feigning unawareness of Rumi's plight, Shems listened to Sultan Veled's assurances that those who opposed him in the past now begged his forgiveness. They wanted him to return for the sake of Rumi's health. Eventually Shems agreed, albeit reluctantly, to accompany Sultan Veled back to Konya.

On a spring day in May 1247 Shems arrived. Town criers were sent out into the street to announce his arrival. The city fathers and Mevlana Jaláluddin Rumi himself passed through the city gates to meet him. Later Rumi recorded the event in a poem:

> He came, friends, my sun and moon arrived.
> My eye, ear, my silver-bodied, gold-skinned beloved
> arrived.
>
> I'm drunk, filled with happiness on this day
> For my tall cypress, the one who caused me to die
> throughout the night.

Shems' return to Konya signalled the beginning of a new round of *sobhets* and *semas*. The two friends burned in the ecstasy of one another's presence. Rumi's increasing maturity as an ascetic demanded that Shems exert more control than he might have done in the past. Between them they were able to inspire each other to levels of mystical gnosis not previously encountered by Moslems. They took the Faith into new areas of revelation, plumbed new depths of *hal*. Indeed their achievements have been surpassed by only a few sages in the entire annals of mysticism. They explored Love's abandonment and the subsequent diminution of the individual ego. At the same time, they experienced Love's super-abundance in the wake of their spiritual prostrations and their desire to fill their souls with knowledge of Him. From this point onward Islam found itself heir to a form of spirituality which eliminated once and for all the gap between man and God, and made union possible. Rumi himself expressed what they had discovered:

> We rejected love, put desire and longing behind us,
> Because love's greatness transcends such yearning.
>
> He who puts to sea is always aboard fear and hope.
> If the boat sinks and the traveller drowns, emptiness
> ripples the ocean.

> He who attaches his heart to a plank of wood for fear of
>   drowning,
> Is no traveller, but a man revolting against his essence.

Hoping to bind Shems to him more securely, Rumi offered him his adopted daughter as his wife. Shems consented. Thus he became a member of Rumi's family, and accordingly received the normal privileges bestowed upon any son-in-law. Far from silencing his critics, however, this act merely revived old animosities, and Shems found himself the butt of many a rumour as people once again began to resent his influence over Rumi.

Nevertheless the two men resumed their *sobhets* together. By this time the monastery doors had been closed to all visitors so that they might struggle to realize in peace the divine joy of union with God. Shems, the teacher and guide, had become the bridge over which Rumi crossed on the road to God. Knowing that his pupil had outstripped him in mystical insight and love, Shems was content to step aside and allow Rumi to receive the grace of divine favour without him. It was enough for him to witness this transformation, this remarkable inclination towards unity that his friend bestowed upon all those who came into contact with him. For Rumi had discovered that to love without expectation or the prospect of repletion, indeed to love every thing, person and creature, was the key to knowing bliss on earth. The fine line between truth and illusion was laid bare by love. As he said: 'To rid yourself of falsehood, you must give yourself up to God. There is no need for either a road to follow or provisions for the journey. Either give up falsehood to reach God, or give yourself up to God in order to rid yourself of falsehood.'

Under Shems' tutelage, Rumi had finally sealed his heart against everything but love, both human and divine. His concern was with God and those who counted themselves as friends of God. Through the *sema* he had brought true faith to the very pitch of love, making love and ecstasy almost palpable in his act of dancing. In his hands the *sema* was carried forward into a state beyond consciousness and reason. Representing the noblest of all intoxications, it assured him of departing momentarily from all constraints of reason, so that he might enter into the final abysm of Love. Shems had been the architect of this transformation; but Rumi alone had drawn forth from the kernel of their friendship a mystical dimension not known to Islam since the days of Mohammed himself.

Such a peerless encounter between two men inevitably provoked Rumi's disciples. It was inconceivable to them that Rumi might find all that he needed in Shems. How could this vagabond fulfil all Rumi's desires? Their resentment soon changed to hate, which in turn caused them to conspire to put an end to the relationship. One evening in December 1247, while Rumi and Shems were talking together in their cell, it was announced that a dervish had come from afar to meet with Shems. Shems rose and left the room to see who the dervish might be. Entering the courtyard, he was immediately set upon by seven men and stabbed to death. His cry, 'My God!' reached Rumi, but too late. By the time he rushed outside to discover what had happened, Shems' body had been carried off into the darkness, later to be thrown down a well. A few blood-stains were said to have remained on the courtyard cobbles as the only clue to the crime, though this could well be hagiographic speculation on the part of the commentators.

Shems' sacrifice signalled the end of the physical phase of their friendship. Although for the rest of his life Rumi continued to believe that Shems had merely disappeared, much as he had done once before, he in fact already recognized that their friendship had entered into an other-worldly condition which could only be expressed through his poetry. The poet in him had come to fruition at last, and Shems alone was responsible for this transformation. But the poet's lot is a solitary one, and Rumi knew that he must set out on the final stage of his interior journey, using the staff of words as his sole aid and companion. Shems' greatest gifts to Rumi, the friend of his life, were the power of intuition and a glorious muscularity of language. By forcing Rumi to step outside the confines of learning, he encouraged the poet to experience life as it is, raw and untamed, a rich ferment of desire and anguish needing to be consumed by the purifying fires of love.

Rumi, for his part, bestowed upon Shems an inner calm. He helped him to quiet his restless ways and submit them to the pure beneficence of love. All his life Shems had been in search of a man who could share his spiritual confidence, as well as bear the brunt of his dynamic personality. He had been looking for a man capable of receiving and imbibing his emotional experience, a man whom he could shake, destroy, build, regenerate and elevate. As *Parindah*, the flier, he had flown like a bird from one country to another in search of such a man. In Mevlana Jaláluddin Rumi he met his master, the one man whose spiritual largesse was such that it might embrace him completely. Shems had shaken the tree, and now the ripened fruit lay on the ground. It was up to Rumi to begin gathering in the harvest.

5

Entering Rumi's mausoleum in Konya on that early winter morning heralded the beginning of my own rich harvest of his poetry and thought. Here indeed was a man who shared my belief in the power of friendship as a vivifying factor between people of sensibility and complementary insight. In an age when mutual respect and love between people of individual destinies has all but been reduced to a plethora of shallow emotions, the prospect of finding exemplars of Rumi and Shems' stature lying among the debris of history filled me with joy. I hoped that, in my knowing them, they might begin to serve as my guides through the hallowed halls of mystical knowledge that lay before me.

The snow outside in the courtyard fretted white the cobbles where once the two friends had walked. The tomb itself was built over the Garden of the Wise Men where Rumi was first interred. A dome of sixteen faces supported by four pillars, it is decorated on the outside with mosaics and on the inside with painted motifs. The wooden sarcophagus, designed by the architect Abdulvahid, is built of walnut on which an inscription from the Koran is carved, together with another singing Rumi's praise:

> ... here is the resting place of Rumi, Sultan of the Wise, shining light of God illuminating the darkness, an imam son of an imam, support of Islam, a guide of the people who leads them into God's glorious presence ...

In the high dome the sound of a reed flute (*ney*) fills the still air. Rumi's dervish hat, placed at the head of the sarcophagus, casts a shadow on the wall behind. Detailed Arabic inscriptions mingle with stylized motifs from nature in the archway above. A brazier makes a rather futile attempt to warm the tomb against the chill outside; while about me pilgrims from all over Turkey pay their respects, softly murmuring their prayers as they file past. All of them, I suspect, harbour a deep longing to experience the bliss of love that this 'Sultan of the Heart' so ably expressed in his life and poetry.

It is true that the love Rumi and Shems bore for one another finds its echoes in other memorable encounters between men. The disposition towards 'giving one's head' for a friend marks a high level of attainment in the conduct of human relationships, and is in itself a sign of high cultural achievement. We acknowledge it as an intrinsic part of the warrior tradition, whether it be between Achilles and Patroclus in *The Iliad*, or two friends who happened to die for one another in the trenches on the Somme. The idea that death hangs as a sword above the *quality* of friendship, ready to rend it in two at the moment of apotheosis, lends a poignancy to the human predicament that no words can properly express.

The word 'friendship' derives its meaning from the old Teutonic word *frijojan* meaning 'to love'. Its pre-Teutonic origins, however, lie in the word *priyo* meaning 'dear', a word which further finds its root in another Teutonic expression, *frio* meaning 'free'. The Old English equivalent for 'free' is *fréon*, meaning 'to love', from which our modern word for 'friend' is derived. Thus we are confronted with a spiritual condition generated between people which is linked to the idea of love and freedom, two qualities perfectly reflected in the lives of Rumi and Shems. Furthermore, the idea of a 'yoking' or 'conjunction' is also implied. By linking oneself with another, or with God through another, friends are able to explore what James Joyce termed a capacity to 'meet ourselves' in that other person as we plumb the depths of fraternity.[5]

Such a perception is given further credence by Marcelio

Ficino, the great Platonic philosopher of the Italian Renaissance, and his friend Giovanni Cavalcante. He regarded friendship as the 'single and permanent virtue of the soul' when he wrote in one of his Letters to Cavalcante that 'the permanent union of lives, which is true friendship, can only exist for those who neither seek to accumulate riches nor satisfy sensual pleasures.' As far as he was concerned, friendship as a spiritual condition was 'forged by God'. It could only be attained by those who were prepared to forsake material expectations in order to pursue the 'whole study and business of Man', which was 'always to strive for what is thought to be good'. Clearly, Shems and Rumi agreed, as their friendship subsequently spawned a voluminous poetic output on Rumi's part in his pursuit of the good.

If we explore history and literature in greater depth, we discover numerous examples of what might be termed the 'nobility of friendship'. Gilgamesh and Enkidu, two Sumerian heroes, fought one another to a standstill before embracing and becoming friends. Defoe described the friendship between Robinson Crusoe and Friday in terms that could only suggest the existence of a deep spiritual bond. After three years of living together on that remote island, Crusoe acknowledges that they had 'achieved perfect and compleat Happiness, if any such Thing as compleat Happiness can be form'd in a sublunary state.' Behind the Protestant reserve of Defoe's prose we see a powerful intimation of the unique and extraordinary nature of friendship. The 'sublunary state' is indeed transformed by any encounter between two people prepared to acknowledge the full dimension of themselves.

For what is at stake in these encounters is the attainment of a stage of knowledge known in Sufi mysticism as *waliyah*, or visionary perception. This can only come about when the essence of truth is learnt through direct experience. It is the stage at which the correspondence between what is perceived and what is known is complete. To enter into this state of *waliyah* (and become, by implication, a *wali* or visionary philosopher) requires the seeker to dedicate himself to the art of friendship with all his will and energy. The path towards mystical gnosis may be long and arduous, but if one is accompanied by a friend who knows then the going becomes a little easier. For the visionary philosopher, in contrast to the philosopher who relies only upon *ratio* (intellectual perception), the task of realizing union with God takes on an entirely new dimension – that of risk, to one's physical being as well as to one's soul. In the case of Shems, 'pledging his head' for the sake of his friend meant that he had to give up his life in order that his friend might be free from his influence.

Freedom is an essential ingredient of fraternity. The minute one partner binds another to himself by way of fear or insecurity, the friendship is doomed. Such an attenuation was a feature of the relationship between the French poets Paul Verlaine and Arthur Rimbaud during the nineteenth century when they chose to become 'fast friends'. Living together in London, sharing their youthful experiences amid the social chaos of England's emerging industrial class, only intensified their resistance to a world already committed to the dehumanizing processes of the factory floor. They observed the shackles of economic constraint imposed on both rich and poor alike, and so their arrogance in the face of such conformity was provoked by despair rather than hubris. It forced Verlaine to cling to Rimbaud, thus ruining the sense of freedom inspired by their initial contact. Their friendship was finally destroyed in a sleazy hotel room in Brussels where Verlaine attempted to shoot Rimbaud because of the humiliation he had experienced at the hands of his erstwhile friend. Their loss of freedom – that fragile flower which only blooms when the conditions are right – had reduced them to the status of peons. Any nobility they had encountered through knowing one another was later destroyed by accusations of betrayal and distrust.

Such freedom did exist, however, between Vincent van Gogh and his brother, Theo. A turbulent career as a religious zealot and later a painter of genius forced Vincent into the arms of his brother for succour. Their friendship was one of loyalty and concern, and of a deep commitment to each other's well-being. Vincent, ever the articulate one, mused on their relationship in a letter to Theo written from Holland in 1883: 'Actually, deep down in you I see the artist, the true artist. You must look upon yourself and me as painters.' At the same time he acknowledged, 'I feel within me a beginning of a change for the better. So I only say that I would not be in the least astonished if, after some time, we were *here* together. I feel that it *may* happen.' Furthermore, 'two persons must believe in each other, and feel that it *can* be done, in that way they are enormously strong. Thus we must keep up each other's courage. Well, I think you and I understand each other.'

Clearly Vincent understood how freely one submits to the other, while at the same time being prepared to give moral support if and when it is required. He also acknowledged the essential unity of their endeavour. His statement, 'You must look upon yourself and me as painters', is a declaration that both he and Theo are one, that they share the same vision, that they counterbalance one another in their mutual desire to make objects transcend their condition through the act of painting them. Vincent's 'Sunflowers' was born out of syzygy between two men who recognized in themselves a need to conquer the ordinariness of existence by way of artistic celebration.

All this suggests that Donne's statement 'no man is an island' is true. Yet Friedrich Nietzsche, the German philosopher, and Richard Wagner, composer of numerous well-known operas, discovered to their cost that abandoning their friendship could only lead to loneliness and moral collapse. What for them began as a heroic bid to preserve the feeling of elevation that invariably accompanies friendship, was finally reduced to a desire to destroy the very premise by which it was engendered. The unquenchable desire for congeniality, for fellowship, eventually turned in upon itself, breeding instead an obsessive need to erase all traces of what was once, for Nietzsche and Wagner at least, one of the pure pedestals of experience. They had set out together as friends of the spirit, only to grow disillusioned with one another because of the extreme philosophic positions they had adopted with regard to their work. Neither wished to give ground, and so they parted. But in parting, they did not separate. For the rest of their lives each mourned the loss of the other, flailing one another in subsequent articles and prose works. After their break, Wagner's wife asked him one day whether he was dissatisfied with life. Wagner replied, 'Not *my* life, but *with* life.'

Years later Nietzsche was still inquiring after Wagner. He wrote: 'I think of him with everlasting gratitude, for it is Wagner to whom I owe some of the most powerful impulses towards spiritual and intellectual independence.' Nevertheless, he acknowledged with sadness the impossibility of resolving their impasse when he recognized, too late, how he had insisted on truth at the expense of love. 'These are the heaviest sacrifices that my life and thought have demanded of me,' he wrote. 'It strikes me as so foolish to insist on being right at the price of love and *not* to be able to impart one's most valuable possessions in order not to remove the friendly feelings.' In marked contrast to Rumi and Shems, Nietzsche and Wagner insisted on maintaining their philosophic and spiritual independence at the expense of their interdependence as friends.

It is clear that what constitutes friendship relies on a capacity for accommodation. Allowing the unique experience of another to become a part of one's own experience forms the web in which friendship is trapped. Singularity of vision can often prove to be a real stumbling block along the path towards union. Drawing upon another's experience and allowing that person's rich personality to influence one's own can provide the backcloth for a shadowplay of complementary attributes which enhance the wonder of knowing each other. Where Rimbaud and Verlaine failed, where Wagner and Nietzsche chose to go their separate ways, where Vincent resolved to abandon life altogether rather than continue loving Theo, Shems and Rumi resorted to a totally different perspective on friendship. They each chose instead to make the other a reflection of God. Their singular personalities became an embodiment of the veil so beloved of Islamic mysticism. Behind it God's countenance lingers, radiant and supreme, waiting to reveal itself to the *wali* who has achieved gnosis.

One of the greatest friendships of our time has been celebrated by the Cretan author Nikos Kazantzakis in his novel *Zorba the Greek*. Many people may not realize that Zorba was, in fact, a living person, a friend of the author. They had met when Kazantzakis had decided to take up a mining lease which he had received as part of his patrimony. Zorba was a free spirit, a vagabond, in the mould of Shems of Tabriz or the troubadour poet, François Villon. He had wandered about Greece and Asia Minor all his life, going wherever his whim took him. Often he had played his *santuri* (a form of harp) in village squares for a few drachma in order to survive. His *santuri* was his portable meditation, the device by which he could transcend himself, much as Shems did while dancing the *sema*. To Zorba, his *santuri* was a 'wild animal' needing freedom. No man owned it, nor could it be put at the disposal of another on demand.

In the course of their friendship, Kazantzakis learned one important lesson which was to serve him well for the rest of his life: that one had to be a little mad in order to live a full life. In contrast, the life of 'boats, machines and neckties' could not, as far as Zorba was concerned, produce the flowers of kindness and honesty. He was wedded instead to a vision of paradise in which true liberty on earth was a reality rather than an aspiration. This liberty, however, evolved not from the rule of law or the comforting embrace of a secure existence, but from a willingness to give up all that one has acquired, or indeed stands for, including friendship itself. A man must have the courage to risk all, and not to listen to the 'shopkeeper's head' in himself which is constantly totting up the profit and loss of life. It was this kind of courage that Zorba imparted to his friend Kazantzakis before they toasted one another on the beach and separated for the last time.

6

'Mind is the conqueror of the Angel. Though the Angel has a definite form and feathers and wings while Mind has not, in reality they are one and the same.' So said Mevlana Jaláluddin Rumi in one of his *Discourses* as he meditated on the likeness of the Angel to man. The angelic presence in a man's life, however, often takes the form of another, a friend who embodies all the virtues that appear to be lacking in himself. The friend, the Angel, becomes a visitant, one who sheds light on the multiplicity of existence through the luminosity of his presence. He embodies a vision of transcendence which might previously have been no more than a vague configuration of ideals which a man might hope to realize at some unspecified time in his life.

The friendship between Rumi and Shems has given us an archetype of unity which neither history nor literature had previously bestowed upon us. Christ's love for his disciples is not one between equals; nor is that between Mohammed and his followers. The relationship between Achilles and Patroclus is more that of a prince and his courtier, as is that between Gilgamesh and Enkidu. It seems that all previous attempts to define friendship in terms of intellectual, emotional and spiritual equality have only partially realized their objective. The first successful example in European literature is probably the relationship between Dante and Virgil, in which Virgil treats Dante as an equal as they make their journey through Hell and Purgatory. Even here, however, there is still some suggestion of a teacher-pupil relationship.

Clearly what is intrinsic to the nature of true friendship is its ability to change the consciousness of those involved.

In the case of Rumi and Shems, we have witnessed the distillation of two individual egos into a drink more potent than either could have brewed alone. When their destinies coincided, we saw the birth of a rich new dimension to the human psyche. No longer did a man need to 'wander where the wind bloweth' in his desperate search for spiritual knowledge. Shems, as the archetypal wanderer, had to be brought down to earth, had to be made to accept stillness as a vital part of his spiritual development. He had to give up, freely, his reliance on the delightful uncertainties of the road if he were to achieve genuine union with God, as distinct from any fleeting insight that may occur. Rumi, on the other hand, was encouraged to break with dogma and certitude, with rational processes, and with the illusory efficacy of unquestioned tradition. He had to be taught to understand the power of feeling, intuition, and the deep longing of the human spirit to engage in dialogue with the divine, not in a formal, verbal sense, but by resorting to the transcendent language of symbols.

The friendship between these men enabled both of them to break with their respective modes of behaviour and thought. Central to their development was their participation in the *sema*, the divine dance which carried them out of themselves into a more rarefied realm. Nor is the ecstatic dance confined to the Mevlana order of dervishes. Many traditional religions, stretching from the Aboriginal corroboree in Australia to the Hindu dances in Bali, testify to the power of the dance as a medium of deific expression. The soul of dance is made up of the invincible differences between the dancers, while its subtle matter consists of the identity of their desires. Thus for the dancers the act of dancing, so divine in its upsurgings and delicate in its lines, brings forth a universal creature which has neither body nor features, but which nevertheless lays before them gifts, days, and destinies. The dance is an act of renewal, a way of reaffirming the pristine nature of the world over the ever-present threat of fragmentation and decay. The *sema* represented for Shems and Rumi the ecstasy and movement of their love for God.

Moreover, the *ney*, or reed flute, which orchestrated the *sema*, was for Rumi the voice of the 'Perfect Man' (*insani kamil*) since, on the non-royal version at least, its seven apertures represented the apertures on the head of man – eyes, ears, nostrils and mouth. When played by a man of spirit, it was capable of whispering God's mysteries. According to tradition, the first *ney* heard by the Prophet David was the impassioned voice of the reeds as he walked near a reedbed. He picked one, put it to his lips and blew. From that day onward he sang of his love for God with this instrument, and it is said that his Psalms were inspired by the sweet sound of the *ney* crying out like a lover. According to Rumi one must 'listen to the complaints of the *ney*, how it tells of separation.' The *ney*, along with the *rebap* and *sema*, are inseparable partners of any rite of union.

7

Shems' death marked the true beginning of Rumi's career as a mystic poet. In the following years he wrote voluminously, completing over 50,000 verses of impassioned lyric poetry which make up the *Divan-i Shems-i-Tabriz* and the *Mathnawi*. Though Rumi lived another twenty-five years after his friend's disappearance, Shems was never far from his thoughts. In the *Divan* he celebrated their friendship in a way that no other relationship has been celebrated, except perhaps that between Dante and Beatrice in Dante's *La Vita Nuova*. No two men adored God through one another as completely as did Shems and Rumi. And no two men were able to refashion themselves in the divine image through one another with such a fine concern for their individual differences.

Rumi's poetry is eclectic in its philosophical origins. He drew from sources outside Islamic culture, including those of Neo-Platonic, Christian, Jewish, Persian and Hindu belief. Possessed by such an overwhelming vision of love, he was unable to confine himself to any one spiritual discipline for his inspiration. Life, the mythic inheritance of all ages, the intermingling of traditions that he saw about him – these formed the bedrock upon which he fashioned his verses. Though he never denied the primacy of his own Islamic faith, he was quick to recognize that the religion of love transcends doctrinal frontiers. In this sense he was a true Sufi, an *urafa* or gnostic. He saw the physical world as a bridge to the Sublime, so that everyday images became for him a reflection of the Divine Other. As a result, the images in his verses often struggle to contain the extreme tension generated by his thoughts.

In defence of his symbolic technique, Rumi acknowledged the truth of an Arabic proverb: 'When the whole of a thing is unattainable, the whole of it should not therefore be relinquished.' In other words, knowing that the whole of a thing is unattainable, one should not refrain from at least attempting a certain approximation. 'Although one cannot drink rain from cloud, one cannot refrain from drinking water either' was the way Rumi explained it. Language, therefore, was not necessarily the ideal mode of expression for mystical experience. Just as the sun's brightness constitutes its most effective veil, so too must a poet invent colourful images in order to reveal to the world how marvellous the sun is. Thus, while the word often veils the extreme beauty of truth, it also intimates the 'divine fire' of truth itself. Allusion, not identification, is the hallmark of Rumi's poetic technique.

The influence of his poetry, particularly that of the *Mathnawi*, has extended throughout the world. In the Indian sub-continent his work was read among various Sufi orders, as well as by certain learned Brahmins. Shems himself has become a well-known figure in Indo-Moslem folk poetry where he is portrayed as a martyr of love. The Emperor Akbar (1556–1605) loved the *Mathnawi*, and we know that Rumi's works were much respected at Shah Jehan's court (ruled 1627–1658). In Kashmir, Afghanistan, Iran, and throughout the Mogul Empire his works were regarded with esteem. Only among Arab countries was his influence far less, due to the extreme differences in style between Arabic and Persian. It was not until the eighteenth and nineteenth centuries that his works were first translated into European languages. The German reading public were quick to appreciate his *ghazals*, which were championed by both Goethe and Hegel. Parts of the *Mathnawi* appeared in English in 1881, translated by the British scholar Sir James Redhouse, but it was not until 1898 that a selection from the *Divan-i Shems-i-Tabriz* was translated into English by the noted orientalist R A Nicholson.

Rumi's genius lay in his acknowledgement of the need for a *pir* or spiritual guide. He maintained that no real life was possible without the mediation of the few elect, the veritable 'men of God', who alone are the true interpreters of Divine Love. His friendship with Shems reflected this ideal: that a man must seek out not only his opposite, but also one capable of guiding him towards an understanding of mystical knowledge. In the end, however, even he admitted that in the final stages of union the master must step aside and allow his pupil to ascend alone, much as Virgil did at the conclusion of Purgatory in the *Divine Comedy*.

Rumi's message is relatively simple, in spite of the enormity of his opus exploring the mystery of humankind's relationship with God. To be a 'fool for God' requires much more of a person than to act without care for the consequences. Although the idea of abandonment to the love of God was central to his belief, he also insisted upon a more rigorous approach to the role of intuition as a mode of perception. He considered the movement of the intellect towards gnosis by way of feeling to be an important register of God's beneficence, and not a lower order of encounter as sometimes claimed. Rumi's pantheism, or more exactly his 'panentheism' (that is, the universal praise of God), was directed towards one supreme goal: the union of humankind with God. For him, his love of all things was but a manifestation of God's love for all humankind.[6] This reciprocation became the cherished ideal of all genuine knowers of God (*'arif bi'llah*). It is further reinforced by a *hadith* (Koranic exegesis or interpretation) which explains God's coming into this world: 'I was a hidden treasure and I longed to be known. So I created the Creation so that I may be known.' In other words, God manifested Himself in the world in order that he might be adored, or to adore Himself.

Here a certain question arises, a question that Rumi was at pains to address: How does a person who has the aptitude for the state of gnosis (*ma'arifa*) begin to understand his own reality? Rumi's answer was that a seeker must first find a guide who knows his own self. Once he has found him, then with all his heart and soul he must transform his character into that of his guide. The person who desires mystical knowledge should hold on to this way and, through his spiritual guide, 'search for the means that will take you to Him'. Another *hadith* explains it well in the words: 'He who knows himself knows his Lord.'

Shems was that guide, transient and yet eternal, the wild, uncompromising spirit of nature, Angel, alter ego and friend. He alone was able to light Rumi's fire, burn him, and extract from him the pure cinders of love. Though he came and then went, though he allowed himself to be martyred, Shems was able, through his restless energy and the gift of his head, to bestow upon the world a new sensibility: that of discovering divine freedom in another. Shems' contribution to the creation of Rumi as a poet of incomparable grandeur and insight is intrinsic. Like Beatrice, Theo van Gogh, and Zorba after him, he instilled vision in another. He was able to prepare the ground for the creation of something fundamentally eternal, something upon which all culture is based – none other than *poema* or poetry, the rendering of Spirit as Word, divine and unalloyed, the language of men as angels.

8

My own translation of the following selection of odes from the *Divan-i Shems-i-Tabriz* is derived from R A Nicholson's parallel text published in 1898. Nicholson's translation is faithful to the meaning of the text, but in my view fails the test of poetry. Little attempt has been made to employ the rhythm or metrical scansion so essential to English poetry. Instead, Nicholson seems to have opted for a literal translation at the expense of the text's inherent verbal dexterity and beauty. In contrast, I have tried to render Nicholson's prose version of Rumi's lines using modern verse structures, believing that readers today are more familiar with these than they are with Victorian diction.

Ultimately the perception of the intellect is given in the word, that of the emotions in cadence. It is only when perfect rhythm is allied to perfect word that the duality of this vision can be recorded. In the interests of clarity I have tried to compress Rumi's discursiveness so that the impact of his poetry is more defined. By breaking the odes down into their original *beyts*, or couplets, I hope that their line of thought becomes less diffuse. Rumi was often haphazard in the use of metaphors, an indication perhaps that he rarely revised after the initial composition. This is likely, given that he normally wrote with the aid of a scribe. One suspects also that he fashioned his poetry in sharp bursts, which occasionally leads to a disconnectedness between couplets. Rather than to translate his work line for line, the challenge has been to embody in the whole of my English some trace of that power which reveals the man himself.

In the history of every great poet there is always something that transcends the merely human. There is about him a sacred presence, a *nomen*, or *numen*, that shivers in the soul whenever his name is mentioned. Rumi's work conforms to the supreme test of poetry because of its loftiness of conception. Lyrical and didactic, edifying and allegorical, it explores both the abstract and the sensual. Great poets abide by one law, that of the exceptional, and this was true also of Rumi. His spiritual adventure, like that of his beloved friend Shems, was one of absolutes, though without departing from the empire of the real. In pursuit of his goal he was not afraid to resort to the carnal, the visual, or even the prosaic, as he set about the task of delineating God's presence in the world, as well as in humankind. Furthermore his language of love put heart back into Persian poetry at a time when it was losing ground to the academics.

Mevlana Jaláluddin Rumi conducted his quest for unity at the frontier of the great free spaces where the divine unfolds. He was able to discover that blinding point of rapture, that momentary cataclysm of insight, of which there is no memory, only allusion. He sought to define this luminous essence through the medium of his friend whose mask he adopted. The memory of Shems became his vehicle and his talisman as he plumbed the depths of the Real. Breathing the breath of the world became his primary function as a poet as he sought to reintegrate man in all his plenary aspiration. Vehement soul that he was, Rumi has given us an indelible picture of the divine working within the spirit of man.

Shems is, of course, the hero of the *Divan*. Many of Rumi's odes are addressed to Shems whom he identifies as the Perfect Man. He is Adam, Moses, Jesus and Mary combined, at once the secret and the revealer of mysteries to man. All bitterness and disappointment is rendered sweet by him. He alone has the power to convert disbelief into faith. Invested with all kinds of paradoxical qualities, it is to him that Rumi turns for guidance, help and support as they scale the spiritual heights together. As Rumi's friend and confidant, master and guide, Shems is at once Noah, the Spirit, the Conqueror and the Conquered. He is light and revelation, mercy, grace and terror. A true paragon, he haunts Rumi's odes, his mysterious presence forever veiled. At times he is God, at other times himself. His role in the odes is that of the divine trickster, forever confusing the reader as to his true identity. This is because the Perfect Man can only reveal himself after years of ascetic practice and prayer.

Ultimately, Shems represents Rumi's primeval consciousness, unburdened with thought and learning. He is the wild spirit that inhabits the non-rational intuitive area of being, not necessarily as a chthonic force wedded to earth, but as that virginal aspect of the soul. Shems is as much the Eternal Feminine as he is the Wild One; the wrestler who longs to engage in combat with the more rational aspect of being in order to temper its overweening desire to dominate the process of spiritual growth. Taken together, Rumi and Shems represent the principle of duality endeavouring to become One, and the entire fragmentary nature of existence yearning for wholeness.

9

Leaving Rumi's mausoleum in Konya at last, along with so
many other pious pilgrims, I was made to realize that he
continues to live on. He is not a mound of dust or a piece
of hagiography that has drifted down to us from the
thirteenth century. The water splashing in the fountain
outside is a perfect metaphor for his existence, suggesting
that his voice with all its indefinable fluidity continues to
stimulate our intellects. I now understood that quantitive
time had been overreached by another form of time – the
time of souls – that time which is discontinuous and
irreducible to the computations of the calendar. I had
encountered Rumi and Shems in the streets of this city
precisely because we had met in the spirit of mutual understanding. Our hearts had met under the clock tower of love
to which all genuine seekers gravitate when they enter an
unknown city.

Prior to making the journey across the Anatolian
steppes, I had not anticipated such a revelation. I would
have been satisfied, I suppose, with a vicarious encounter,
whereby I might have rubbed shoulders for a short while
with two seers from the past. But to discover that Rumi and
Shems underwent a spiritual initiation which invested
human meaning with a sacred beauty made me realize
how far and yet, paradoxically, how close I was to such an
initiation myself. Authentic love (*ishq hagiqi*), the love of
one soul for another, draws together two modes of being,
the Lover and the Beloved. An anonymous glossarist from
the Safavid period put it well when commenting on the
mystical lover, Majnun, and his relationship with Layla: 'I
am whom I love; whom I love is me; we are two spirits

immanent in a single body.' It is clear that what occurred between Rumi and Shems was a metamorphosis of human love into divine love. In them 'God himself [who], by his own eternal gaze, contemplated his own eternal face.' They had become, in a sense, the eyes of God gazing at Himself.

I had set out to discover my own secret, and had inadvertently done so. As exemplars, Rumi and Shems had pointed the way – and indeed still do so. Their friendship is immediately real, and is made up of a transfiguring beauty. They have passed the supreme test, the test of the veil, and in the process have mapped unknown territory for those terrestrial pilgrims such as myself who follow in their footsteps. I now knew how Ruzbehan Baqli of Shiraz (1128–1209) must have felt when he confessed: 'Thus I remained in between, between separation and reunion, and there was no place where I could flee nor refuge where I could weep.'[7] Except, perhaps, to flee towards a friendship with these two men from the steppes of Turkey – two men who had discovered that there is no limit to what human relationships have to offer, provided they are measured against the relationship we have with God.

James Cowan

Notes

1   The name given to the Roman Empire in the East. It was used later to describe the Ottoman Empire which succeeded the Byzantine and Seljuk period of occupation of Anatolia.

2   The Assassins were a fanatical Syrian sect that achieved an unsavoury reputation as political murderers during the time of the Saracens.

3   The Ismaeli and Sunni sects represent the two principal sects of Islam. They trace their origins to the period after the Prophet's death when the question of spiritual succession was hotly contested. In the end, the followers of Ali, the Ismaelis, found themselves oppressed by the politically and numerically stronger Sunnis. Today Iran remains the centre of Ismaeli belief, while most of Africa and the Middle East is Sunni.

4   It is interesting to compare Dante's encounter with Beatrice: 'The moment I saw her I say in all truth that the vital spirit, which dwells in the inmost depths of the heart, began to tremble so violently that I felt the vibration alarmingly in all my pulses, even the weakest of them.' (Translated by Barbara Reynolds, Penguin Classics, 1969.) Such a spiritual encounter quite obviously presages a physical as well as an intellectual reaction. Love may be at the root of this encounter, whether it be between opposing sexes or otherwise.

5   Joyce wrote of it thus: 'Every day in many ways, day after day, we walk through ourselves, meeting robbers, ghosts, giants, old men, young men, wives, widows, brothers-in-law. But always meeting ourselves.'

6   Compare these words by Simon of Taibutheth: 'Consider, O discerning man, that you are the image of God and the bond of all creation, both of the heavenly and of the terrestrial beings, and whenever you bend your head to worship and

glorify God, all the creations, both heavenly and terrestrial, bow their heads with you and in you, to worship God; and whenever you do not worship and glorify Him, all the creations grieve over you and turn against you, and you fall from grace.' (Woodbrook Studies, vol. VII, Cambridge, 1934.)

7 The full text from Ruzbehan's *Book of the Clouding-Over* reads:

'Oh! what a small boy is he who sees the moon at the summit of the mountain and imagines that when he has climbed the summit, he can seize the moon. How could he seize it? The moon is even beyond Mt Qaf [the cosmic mountain] ... I have contemplated the new moon of Unity, but a pre-eternal jealousy has prevented me from reaching it by a cloud. Thus I remained in between, between separation and reunion, and there was no place where I could flee nor refuge where I could weep.' (*'The Jasmine of the Fideli D'Amore'*, Henry Corbin, *Sphinx Magazine*, vol. 3, 1989.)

The Odes

If you're Love's lover and seek Love
Cut modesty's throat with a knife.

Know that renown hinders insight;
And, thinking clearly, understand.

Did the madman reveal his madness?
Did he, the Wild One, display his guile?

He tore his clothes, climbed mountains,
Drank poison and chose death.

Like a spider seizing its victim, the Lord
Is capable of seizing us in his web!

Only Laila's face embodies such love
So why did the Wild One leave us?

Have you read the divans of Waisa and Ramin
The stories of Wamiq and Adra?

You raise your clothes for fear of wetting them
Knowing that into the sea you must plunge.

Depravity and drunkenness are Love's way
As torrents descend rather than rise.

You will be a rock in a ring of lovers
The stone's slave as we are yours.

Even as the sky enslaves the earth
Even as the spirit enslaves the body.

What does the earth lose by being bound
As limbs are by the sweetness of reason?

Don't beat a drum under your blanket,
Brave man, plant your banner in the desert.

Soul, listen to all the innumerable sounds
Echoing like a lover's lament in a green dome.

When the buttons on your shirt burst open
Know it's caused by the drunkenness of Love.

Behold, Heaven's triumph, and Orion's surprise!
How the world over is troubled by Love

Yet purified throughout, just as the sun
Slays night, and affliction trails after joy.

I am silent. Speak, Wild One, whose face
Every atom in the universe adores.

2

Our desert has no limit
Our hearts and souls no rest.

World within worlds, we've adopted
His Image – but in what Form?

Seeing on the track a severed head
Rolling towards our field,

Ask of it the heart's secret
If you wish to learn our mystery.

How would it be if an ear revealed
Its knowledge of the singers' notes?

How would it be if a bird took flight
Wearing Solomon's secret on its collar?

What can I say, or think? For this tale
Flies beyond every limit we set ourselves.

Or remain silent when every moment
Pain festers, and become anguish?

Together falcon and partridge fly
Through the clear air of our mountains,

Through the air of Seventh Heaven
Towards Saturn's zenith. Are not

These heavens below the empyrean
With our orbit circling beyond this?

What room is there here for our desire
To ascend towards the empyrean, or sky?

Our journey is towards the rose-garden
Of union, where buds become blooms.

So forget this story. Don't ask us
To complete what is unfinished.

Salahu'Ihaq u din will soon tell you
Of the beauty of our Sultan, King of Kings.

3

Last night I pleaded with a star to intercede:
I said, 'My being is at the moon's service.'

Bowing, I added, 'Take this plea to the sun
Who makes rocks gold with his fire.'

Bearing the wounds on my breast, I cried,
'The Beloved, Whose drink is blood, must know!'

Like a child, I rocked my heart asleep
As a child does when its cradle sways.

Give my heart milk, stay its tears – you
Who help a hundred like me at every moment.

The heart's home is your city of union:
How long will you condemn mine to exile?   ⌐

My head aches; there's nothing more I can say.
O cup-bearer, my troubled eye grows drunk!

4

David said: 'Since you don't need us
Was it wise to create two worlds?'

God replied: 'I was a hidden treasure
Whose Love and Grace needed to be known.

'A mirror's face is the heart, its back the world –
Knowing the back is enough, if the face is unseen.'

When straw is mixed with clay, can a mirror
Be clear? Part them and the mirror shines.

To make grape-juice into wine, it needs to ferment
A while. Brightening your heart takes much effort.

'Whenever my soul leaves my body, my King says:
"You come and go, but where are my gifts?" '

It's well known that alchemy makes copper into gold;
Ours has been transmuted by your sweet alchemy.

By God's grace the Wild One wants no crown or robe,
He's cap to a hundred bald men, cloak to ten naked.

Child, on an ass Jesus sat for humility's sake:
How else could the wind ride on an ass's back?

O Spirit, make your inquiring mind like river-waters.
O Reason, immortality comes from walking daily towards
    death.

Remember God until you forget your self, and be
Lost in the Called, undistracted by caller or call.

5

In a garden, may a rose to Resurrection bloom!
About an idol, may two worlds wreathe his beauty!

The Prince rides forth to hunt in the morning;
May our hearts be wounded by the arrow of his eye!

What messages pass between his eye and mine!
May my eye be heartened by his embrace!

I broke down an ascetic's door: with a prayer
He denounced me, 'Go, may peace never grace one day of
    your life!'

Because of his prayer, no peace nor courage remains.
The Wild One thirsts for my blood, in God's name!

Like the moon, my body melts for Love;
Its strings are broken like Zuhra's lute!

Don't look at the moon waning, at Zuhra's broken state:
Watch the sweetness of his affliction wax like flame.

In the soul a bride! Her face reflects
A world freshly hennaed like nuptial hands.

Don't look at the youth who is liable to decay
But at his spirit, eternal in its grace!

The body is a raven, a wintered world;
Let eternal Spring banish these shades!

For they are fuelled by the four elements:
May our lives depend on more than these!

6

O, You my soul's comfort in this season of sorrow,
O, You my spirit's treasure in the bitterness of loss!

What can't be conceived nor understood
Enters my soul when I worship You.

O King, with Your help my loving gaze is fixed on
        eternity,
Except when what perishes leads me astray.

Unsummoned, the favour of he who brings
Your news more than song rings in my ears.

Knees bent in prayer, the thought of you O Lord
Binds me more than the seven verses.

To You belong mercy and intercession for the sin of
        disbelief:
For me, You're still Lord of the hard-hearted.

If an unlimited bounty should offer kingdoms,
If a buried treasure should grant me gems,

I would bow my soul low, lay my face in the dust
And plead, 'Grant me instead the Love of God!'

For me, eternal life is the time of union
Because in this place time has no substance.

Life is a jug, union the wine within;
Without You, their anguish offers me little.

Before this I had a myriad desires;
Yet my passion for him made me risk all.

By his grace I'm saved, the unseen King's
Words assure: 'You're the soul of the world.'

His essence has filled my heart and soul;
'Au!' cries the cur, denying me a split second.

At the time of union my body dismissed
The spirit; his invisibility filled my gaze.

Though I grew old with his affliction, all
My youth returned when Shems was named.

7

That moon, undreamt even by sky, returns
Bringing a fire no water can quench.

The temple of my body and my soul
Are made drunken and desolate by his love.

When the tavern-keeper became my soul-mate
My blood turned to wine, my heart to kebab.

When the eye is consumed by thought of him
A voice arrives: 'Well done, O Flagon. Bravo, wine!'

Love's fingers drag up, root and stem,
Every flower where Love's rays fall.

When my heart noticed Love's sea, suddenly
It escaped me and leapt in, crying, 'Save me!'

Tabriz's glory, the face of the Wild One is
The Sun whose track all cloudy hearts follow.

8

The man of God remains drunk without wine,
The man of God is replete without meat.

The man of God is distraught and confused,
The man of God is hungry and fatigued.

The man of God is a king in pauper's clothes,
The man of God is a treasure in a ruin.

The man of God is neither air nor earth,
The man of God is not of fire nor water.

The man of God is a boundless ocean,
The man of God rains pearls on a clear day.

The man of God has countless moons and skies,
The man of God has unnumbered suns.

The man of God draws wisdom from truth,
The man of God learns without books.

The man of God is beyond unbelief and religion,
To the man of God right and wrong are the same.

The man of God has escaped from un-being,
The man of God is waited on in glory.

Wild One, the man of God is in hiding,
You look for the man of God everywhere!

9

At every instant Love calls from near and far.
Our destination is Heaven: why dally as tourists?

We've been to Heaven, our friends are angels;
So let's hurry back to where we belong.

We're higher than Heaven, and greater than angels;
Why not pass beyond these? Our goal is Majesty.

How different is dust's source, and the world of pure
    substance!
Though we've come down, let's rise again!

Fortune is our friend, yielding up soul our task;
Our caravan leader is Mustafa, glory of the world.

The wind's sweet smell comes from his curly hair,
This thought's radiance from a cheek 'as bright as the
    morning'.

Cut by his cheek, the moon turned away;
Such is her fortune – while in her heart beggared.

In our hearts this unending 'cleaving of the moon'
Allows knowledge of that vision to transform us.

Came the wind billowing, 'Am I not?' to wreck my
    foundering body;
When it founders again union is attained.

Like waterfowl, men leap up from the sea – that soul's
    ocean;
Coming from that sea, why should any bird make this
    place his haven?

We're all pearls in that sea where we live;
Otherwise, why does wave follow wave from the ocean
    depths?

This is the time of union, when eternity reveals its beauty,
The time of charity and gifts, the ocean of perfect purity.

The wind of giving blows, the thunder of the ocean breaks,
In the morning felicity dawns, a light of God on the
    horizon.

Who is this visible form, this Monarch this Prince?
Who is this ageless wisdom? All veils.

To part a veil requires ecstasies like these
Sprayed from a fountain in your heart.

In the mind alone it's not enough, owning two;
One of clay and earthbound, the other derived purely
    from Heaven.

O, how many clear minds lie beneath clay
Knowing their wisdom depends on the mind of that
    Other!

The first mind lies hidden, the second unveiled,
Just as this world obscures those realms which are
    infinitely present.

O cup-bearer, tie up the skin! Fetch wine:
The jar of insight is filled with a pure draught.

From Tabriz shone the Sun of Truth, so I said:
'Wild One, this light joins all things yet is apart.'

10

What pearl are you that none can buy?
What does the world own that's not your gift?

Is there worse punishment than being exiled from your
    light?
Don't condemn him who is unworthy of you, your servant.

He who has fallen among a whirlpool of accidents
Can't escape by swimming, since he's not your friend.

Without permanence the world perishes,
Being unfamiliar with yours.

How happy the king mated by your rook!
What good company is he who lives for you!

Each day I desire to throw my heart and soul at your feet;
Throw mourning dust on my soul, not dust from your
    feet!

All birds that desire you are blessed;
Those birds that don't are doomed.

I will not avoid your blow, for crude is the heart
Not tempered by the fire of your affliction.

There's no end to those who praise you; what
Atom can resist the sweetness of your word?

Just as Nizami sings in his verse:
Don't tyrannize me as I can't endure it.

O Shems, Wild One, horizon's beauty and glory,
What king's heart is but a beggar of yours?

11

O Beloved, beauty of spirit is glorious,
Yet your loveliness makes me breathless!

O you who have spent years describing spirit
Show me one quality equalling its essence.

At the thought of him my eyes light up
But they fade in the presence of his unity.

I stand open-mouthed, adoring that beauty:
'God is Great' is on my lips at every moment.

My heart's eye longs to see you unceasingly.
Oh, how this need feeds my heart and eye!

Caressing a slave your love has practised;
Since where is the heart worthy of such love?

Every heart that has slept a night in your air
Awakens radiant as day: so the air is illumined.

Everyone who desires nothing is your disciple:
He gains that which resembles no object.

Consumed by the fire of this love, every
Reprobate has fallen into the hell of yours.

Union alone stops my foot touching earth:
Cut off from you, my hand reaches for my head.

O heart, don't be sad at this defeat of enemies,
Think only that the Sweetheart remains judge.

If my opponents rejoice at my sallow face,
Know that this face blooms from a red rose.

Since my Beloved's beauty defies description,
How plump is my grief, how lean my praise!

There's a rule which applies to a man who's ill:
The more pain he feels, the less he complains!

Shine, O Wild One, moon from Tabriz,
Your face erases all lunar expression.

12

Every form derives its nature from the void;
If a form dies, its eternal nature will survive.

Every beauty witnessed, every thought heard,
These will not be trampled upon or perish.

The spring's source is unfailing, its streams offer
    unlimited water;
Since neither can cease, why are you crying?

Regard the soul as a fountain, all creation as rivers:
While the fountain flows forth, rivers swell.

Dismiss grief from your mind and drink your fill;
This spring will not cease, its waters are eternal.

From the moment of your birth a ladder
Was placed before you to help you escape.

First you were mineral, a plant, then animal:
There's no secret about your evolution.

Later you became man, equipped with knowledge, reason
    and faith;
Look at your body, nature's dust-pit, how perfect it has
    grown!

Leaving manhood behind, there's no doubt you'll become
    an angel;
The earth you'll leave then, and head for Heaven.

Transcending the angel, become an ocean
Whose each drop will be larger than countless Seas of
    'Oman.

With all your soul put behind you 'Son', adore instead
   'One';
It doesn't matter how your body ages, your soul's young.

13

A spirit not wearing true Love as a coat
Better not have existed: its cloth is worn.

Be drunk on Love, for only Love exists; there's
No meeting the Beloved without Love as herald.

They ask, 'What's Love?' Reply, 'Renouncing the will.'
He who hasn't tossed will aside doesn't know God.

The lover is a monarch: two worlds lie at his feet;
The King pays no attention to what lies under his.

It's Love and the lover that live eternally;
Set your heart on this only: the rest is borrowed.

How long will you embrace a dead lover?
Embrace the soul which is embraced by nought.

What was born of Spring, in Autumn dies,
Love's rose-garden is not helped by early Spring.

In Spring, the thorn comes as companion to the rose,
Just as grape-juice is not free from headache when wine.

Don't be an expectant observer on this path;
In God's name, there's no death worse than waiting.

Set a price on your heart in sterling, not counterfeit;
Lacking an ear-ring, give ear to this truth.

Don't fear the horse of your body, travel lightly on foot;
God gives wings to the one who finally dismounts.

Dismiss worry and make your heart clear,
A mirror reflecting neither picture nor image.

Devoid of images, all images are contained;
A face is not ashamed, gazing at clarity's face.

Look at yourself! A clear mirror
Is not afraid of reflecting the truth.

A face of steel becomes pure by discrimination,
The heart's face requires nought, it attracts no dust.

Between steel and the heart there's a difference:
One retains secrets, the other none.

14

He asked: 'Who is at the door?' I replied: 'Thy humble
slave.'
He asked: 'Why are you here?' I replied: 'To greet you,
Lord.'

He asked: 'How long will you push?' I replied: 'Until you
call me.'
He asked: 'How long will you glow?' I said: 'Until the
resurrection.'

Thus did I lay claim to Love, taking oaths
That for Love I had given up all sovereignty.

He said: 'Regarding your claim, a judge demands
witness.'
I replied: 'Tears are mine, my pale face I submit as
evidence.'

He said: 'The witness is invalid; your eye corrupt.'
I replied: 'By your majesty, they're clear of sin.'

He asked: 'What are your intentions?' I replied:
'Constancy and friendship.'
He asked: 'What do you want of me?' I replied: 'Your
universal grace.'

He asked: 'Who was your friend?' I replied: 'The thought
of you, O King.'
He asked: 'Who called you here?' I replied: 'The odour of
your cup.'

He asked: 'Where is it most pleasant?' I replied: 'In the
   Emperor's palace.'
He asked: 'What did you see there?' I replied: 'A hundred
   miracles.'

He asked: 'Then why is it so desolate?' I replied: 'For fear
   of the robber.'
He asked: 'Who is the robber?' I replied: 'This feeling of
   blame.'

He asked: 'Where is it safe?' I replied: 'In abstinence and
   piety.'
He asked: 'What is piety?' I said: 'The path to salvation.'

He asked: 'Where is calamity?' I said: 'In the
   neighbourhood of your Love.'
He asked: 'How do you live there?' I said: 'In
   steadfastness.'

Subjecting you to a long trial, it helped me little;
Repentance shines on him who tests one already tested.

O peace! If I should shout aloud his mysteries
Neither door nor roof would restrain you.

15

Ask of the master what house is this
Where a violin's notes are constantly heard.

What does idolatory mean, if this is the Ka'aba's haven?
What does the light of God mean, if this is a Magian
    temple?

In this house lies a treasure the universe can't hold;
This house and master are all acting and pretence.

Don't lay hand on this house, for it's a sanctuary;
Don't speak with the master: last night he drank too
    much!

The dust and rubbish in this house is all musk
And perfume; the roof and door all verse and music.

In truth, whoever finds his way into this house
Is Sultan of the world and Solomon of his time.

O Master, bend your head low from this roof,
For in your clear face I see a token of good luck.

The sight of your face I swear is enough
To dismiss the kingdom of earth as mere fable.

Even the garden is confused, not knowing leaf from
    flower;
Nor are birds able to distinguish snare from bait.

Such is the Lord's haven surrounded by planets,
The house of Love unbounded by gravity's orbit.

The soul mirrors your image in its heart;
The tip of your curl is combed even deeper.

Just as women cut their hands in Joseph's presence,
Come to me, O soul, for the Beloved has joined us.

All those in the house are dead drunk, and ignorant
Of each man who enters, calling out his name.

Don't sit drunk at the door: enter quickly;
He sits in the dark whose place is the threshold.

Those drunk on God, though many, are one;
Those drunk on lust, though alone, are others.

Don't fear a lion's attack when you walk in the forest;
Fear, like thought, is a pure figment of women.

There is not dangerous: all is mercy and Love,
Imagination is the bar that locks your door.

Set fire to the forest, remain silent, O heart,
And hold your tongue, for your tongue is harsh.

16

Reveal your face, as I long for orchard and rose-garden;
Open your lips, as I hunger for the sweetness of sugar.

O Sun, reveal your face from the veil of cloud,
I want to see the glow of its countenance.

Loving you, I heard the sound of the falconer's drum
And flew back, the Sultan's arm the perch I longed for.

'Don't bother me. Go!' you said with all capriciousness;
I long to hear you say again and again, 'Don't bother
    me.'

All the door-keeper's airs and graces I desire
When he orders me, 'Leave, he's not at home.'

O sweet wind, blowing from the Friend's flower-pot,
Blow on me, for I desire news of the basil.

The bread and water of destiny are as treacherous as
    flood-water;
I'm a great fish that longs for the Sea of 'Oman.

Like Jacob, my tears of grief know no limit,
It's Joseph of Canaan's gentle face I desire most.

By God, without you this city is a prison,
Mountain and desert seduce me instead.

In one hand a wine-cup, in the other my Beloved's curl:
To dance in the market-place is what I long for.

My heart wearies of my weak-spirited friends;
I long for Rustam, Lion of God, son of Zal.

Everyone owns some sliver of beauty;
Show me the mine where loveliness is quarried.

Though bankrupt, I'll not accept a small carnelian;
The whole mine of gem-stone is what I want!

Those people who weep and complain tire me;
Give me the drunkard's dribblings any day!

Pharaoh's tyranny has exhausted my soul, son of
    Imran
I long to see the light shine from Moses' face.

They said, 'He's not to be found, we've looked for him
Everywhere.' Yet what can't be found I long for.

My tongue is more eloquent than the nightingale's,
Though envy seals it the moment I cry out.

Last night, the Master wandered abroad with a lantern,
Crying, 'I'm tired of devil and beast. Give me a man!'

My condition transcends all yearning and desire;
Quitting Being and Place leads me to the Essence.

He hides from our sight, and from Him all emanates;
My beacon is the Hidden One, Whose works are
    visible.

My ear heard the tale of faith and was transported;
Say, 'Limbs, body, and the form of faith beckon me.'

I'm Love's recollection, and Love is a fond memory;
I'm consumed by the hand, breast and Othman's pure
    modulation.

My memory is saying, 'At this moment the mercy
Of the Merciful favours me with its passion.'

O cunning minstrel, with the rest of this ode
Confuse me, for it is such confusion I adore.

O Sun, glory of Tabriz, display the dawn of Love;
I'm the hoopoe yearning for Solomon as I wing home.

17

On that day I lived when Names did not,
Nor any sign of existence given identity.

By me Names and the Named were revealed,
On that day when they were neither 'I' nor 'We'.

A sign, the tip of the Beloved's curl, became a pure point
    of revelation;
As yet the tip of that fair curl was not.

Cross and Christian, everywhere I looked;
No Cross sustained his limp and wounded body.

I journeyed to pagan temple and ancient pagoda;
No trace of Him was visible there.

I climbed Herat and Canahar; neither
High hill nor valley harboured His Body.

Fixed in my purpose, I climbed Mount Qaf;
All I discovered was Anqa's prickly nest.

I whipped the reins of search towards the Ka'aba;
Not in that place for young and old did I find Him.

I questioned Ibn Sina about His condition;
He transcended even his worthy intellect.

I journeyed to the place of two bow-lengths;
He was not in that exalted court.

Then I gazed into my own heart
Where I saw Him; He was nowhere else.

Except pure-hearted Shems, Wild One, none
Ever attained his drunkenness or anguish.

18

Before you, the soul grows and decays each hour;
For the sake of one soul can we plead its cause?

Wherever you set foot on earth a mind shoots forth;
For the sake of one mind, should any dispense with you?

When the soul swoons in rapture at your fragrance –
The soul knows the fragrance of the Beloved.

As soon as your scent slips from the mind
The head heaves a hundred sighs, every hair crying.

I have emptied my house, to be quit of all chattels,
Though I wane, your love waxes like flame.

To gamble away the soul for such a gain is best.
Peace! Its worth, O Wild One, exceeds all odds.

In pursuit of your Love, Shems of Tabriz,
My soul scuds like a ship in a fair wind.

19

At dawn a moon appeared from the waves
And ascended, gazing down at me. Then,

Like a falcon snatching a bird in flight,
It snatched me up and flew away.

When I looked up I no longer saw myself:
Into that moon my body had eased, by grace

Of the soul in which I travelled, moon-driven
Until the secret of God's revelation halted me.

Nine spheres of Heaven had merged in that moon;
And the sea washed over the ship of my being,

Breaking against me in waves. Again Wisdom's
Voice boomed; as it happens so it occurs.

At every foam-fleck of the ocean a figure
Emerged and slowly disappeared, just as

My foam-flecked body, receiving a sea-sign,
Melted within and slowly turned to spirit.

Without the regal power of Shems of Tabriz,
Holding the moon or becoming the sea are dreams.

20

Grab the hem of his favour, before he escapes;
Don't draw him like an arrow, or he'll flee the bow.

What disguises he wears, what tricks he invents!
If he appears in one shape, as spirit he slips the snare.

When you seek him above, he shines like the moon in
     water;
When you enter the water he flees skyward.

When you seek him in the placeless, he guides you to
     place.
When you seek him in place, he guides you to the
     placeless.

Like the bird of your imagination, know that the Absolute
Flees from the Imaginary with the speed of an arrow.

Weariness doesn't make me flee trivial things,
Only fear that Beauty will abandon trivialities.

As the wind I am fleet-footed, loving the rose reduces me
     to a breeze;
In Autumn the rose withers in the garden.

His name escapes when an attempt is made to capture it in
     words,
So that you can't say, 'Such a one has flown.'

He flees from you, and if you paint his portrait
His image flies from the canvas, his impression from your
     soul.

21

All night beauty teaches love-lore to Venus and the moon,
By their witchery its eyes seal those of Heaven.

Observe your hearts, O Moslems! Whatever happens
I'm so consumed in him that no heart is consumed by me.

His Love bore me first, and I gave my heart to him at last;
When fruit springs from a branch, on that branch it
    hangs.

The tip of his curl says, 'Hah! Off to rope-dancing.'
The candle of his cheek says, 'Show me a moth to burn.'

O heart, stop dancing on that rope, become a hoop
    instead;
Throw yourself against the flame when his candle is lit.

Once you've known the rapture of burning, you'll never
    survive without his flame;
If the water of life should douse you, his flame will dry
    your spirit.

22

Said someone, 'Master Sana'i is dead.'
The death of such a master is no small thing.

He was not chaff blowing in the wind,
Nor was he water which freezes in winter.

He was not a comb broken by unruly hair,
Nor was he seed which the soil crushed.

He was a treasure of gold in this dust-pit
Who valued the two worlds as a barley-corn.

The earthly flame he flung to earth,
Soul and intellect he bore to Heaven.

That pure elixir mingled with wine-dregs
Rose to the surface, and the sediment settled.

The second soul unknown to most
By God! he surrendered to the Beloved.

Dear friend, in travel it's possible to meet
Men of Marv and of Rai, Roman and Kurd.

Yet each man eventually returns home;
How could satin be matched with wool?

Remain silent as compass points; your name
The King has erased from the book of speech.

23

No favour was left that his beauty did not bestow.
It's not our fault his gifts to you were unrewarding.

You find yourself abused, tyrannized by charm;
In this world, doesn't the fair one play the tyrant?

His love is like sugar, though he gave no sweetness;
His beauty is perfect faith, though he was unfaithful.

Show me a house not lit by him with lamps.
Show me a portico his face hasn't filled with loveliness.

When the spirit was lost in contemplation, it said:
'Only God has contemplated the beauty of God.'

This eye and that lamp are individual lights;
No one could distinguish them when they merged.

Each of these metaphors explains and deceives;
By the morning splendour God revealed, in envy of the
    expression of light on his face.

Never did Destiny, the tailor, stitch a shirt
To anyone's measure. He tore it in pieces.

Shems' sunny face, O glory of all horizons! When
It shone on things perishable made them eternal.

24

When my bier is carried on the day of my death
Don't think my heart remains in this world.

Don't weep for me or cry, 'Woe! Woe!'
Such sadness is the devil's snare.

When you see my hearse, don't cry, 'He's gone, gone!'
Remember, union and encounter are mine in that hour.

When you commit me to the grave, don't say: 'Goodbye,
    goodbye.'
The grave is a curtain concealing the community of
    Paradise.

After looking upon descent, consider resurrection;
To the sun and moon, is setting a calamity?

To you death is a setting; in truth it's a rising.
Though the grave seems like a prison, it comes as the
    soul's release.

What seed buried in earth doesn't grow?
Why doubt the growth of the seed in man?

What bucket lowered doesn't come up brimming?
Why should the spirit's Joseph complain at the well?

Shut your mouth on this side of death, open it beyond.
Your song will be triumphant in nowhere's air.

25

Look on me, you who are my grave's companion,
On the night when you pass from shop and house.

You shall hear me cry out from the tomb, and know
Your presence was never far from my lively gaze.

As reason and intellect I'm within your heart,
At times of gladness, at times of distress.

Strange is the night when you hear a familiar voice
Escape the nip of an asp, or leap from an ant's bite!

As a gift, Love's intoxication will bring to your grave
Wine and mistress, candle and meats, sweets and incense.

At the hour when Intellect's lamp is lit, what cries
Of praise go up from dead men in their tombs!

The dark earth of the graveyard is confounded by their
noise,
By the din of Resurrection's drums, by the pomp of those
risen.

They have torn their shrouds, and closed their ears in
horror.
What is the mind and ear before the blast of this trumpet?

Look into your own eye, and make no mistake,
So that essence of seer and seen become one.

On whatever side you gaze, you shall see my form,
Whether you gaze upon self, or the mass that is visible.

Shun distorted vision and heal your sight, for the evil eye
Will be distant from my beauty in that moment.

Beware, lest in error you see me in human form,
For the spirit is extremely subtle, Love is jealous.

What room is there for form, if what is felt extends
  beyond?
The soul's mirror reflects light that illuminates the world.

Had they looked for God instead of food and livelihood
Not a single blind man seated by the moat would be seen.

Since you have opened a shop in our city as a dealer in
  amorous glances,
Then like light, deal out glances with closed lips.

I hold my peace and keep those who are unworthy in the
  dark;
You are all that is worthy: though for me the mystery is
  forever veiled.

Like the Sun of Tabriz, rise, rise towards the east;
See the star of victory, and the conqueror's banner!

26

From the heart of the Self a scent of the Beloved
  continually drifts:
Why shouldn't I sniff Self into my heart each night?

Last night in God's garden I dreamed: as the sun
Shone forth from my eye, a river of tears flowed.

Each smiling rose springing forth from his lips
Had escaped the thorn of being, and avoided
  Mohammed's sword.

Every tree and grass-blade was dancing in the field,
Though for most people they seemed unmoved.

Suddenly on one side our beloved Cypress appeared,
The garden was in ecstasy, the plain clapped hands.

A face like fire, wine and love aflame – all three
  incandescently aglow;
Because of the mingling of these fires, my soul cried out,
  'Where shall I flee?'

There's no room for Nought in the realm of Divine Unity,
Knowing that in the realm of Number, Nought thrives.

You may count a thousand sweet apples in your hand;
But if you want to make One, crush them all together.

Look! What is this language of the heart when we dismiss
  all letters?
As a quality, colour's purity stems from the source of
  action itself.

O Shems, seated on your throne, before you
All my rhymes are ranked like willing servants.

27

If a tree could fly or walk, how could it suffer
The teeth of a saw, or the blows from an axe?

If the sun did not walk or wane every night,
Would the world be illumined come dawn?

If saltwater didn't rise from sea to sky,
How would the garden be quickened by rain?

When a drop quit home and later returned,
It found a shell and became a pearl.

Didn't Joseph leave his father, and make a tearful journey?
Didn't he find fortune, a kingdom and victory?

Didn't Mustafa make pilgrimage to Medina, gain
Sovereignty, become Lord of countless lands?

Though you haven't feet, choose to trek within yourself,
Like the ruby, receive an imprint from the sun.

O Master, make a journey out of self, into Self.
On such a journey the earth becomes a quarry veined with
     gold.

Yield up sweetness from what is bitter and sour,
Just as rows of grapes spring up from briny soil.

From the Sun, Tabriz's pride, behold these miracles,
Every tree acquires beauty from the light of his warmth.

28

At midnight I cried out, 'Who is this house of the heart?'
He replied, 'It is I, whose face shames the moon and sun.'

He asked, 'Why is your house of the heart so filled with
    images?
I replied, 'Each is a reflection of you, whose face is more
    radiant than a candle from Chigil.'

He asked, 'What's this other image, besmirched with
    heart's blood?'
I replied, 'An image of me, my feet leaden with mud.'

The neck of my soul I bound and brought to him as a
    token:
It's the confidant of Love; don't sacrifice your own friend.

He gave me the end of a thread full of mischief and guile.
'Pull,' he said, 'that I may pull, yet not break it as I do.'

From the soul's tent emerges my Beloved's form, more
    beautiful than ever;
I reached out and he struck my hand, saying, 'Let go!'

I replied: 'You're harsh, like such a one.' 'Know,' he said,
'It's for your own good, not because of anger or spite.'

Whoever enters saying, 'It's me,' hit him on the head;
This is the shrine of love, fool! It's not a sheep-pen.

Surely Salahi dil u din is the image of perfect beauty;
Wipe your eyes, see for yourself this rare image of the
    heart.

29

Why doesn't the soul fly, when from your glorious
    Presence
A speech of such sweet favour comes, saying, 'Arise'?

Why shouldn't a fish leap from dry land into the water
When wave-sounds from the ocean curl in its ear?

Why shouldn't a falcon fly from its kill to be near the King
When it hears drum-stick against drum chatter, 'Return'.

Shouldn't every Sufi dance like a speck of dust on the sun
Of eternity, that he might be delivered from decay?

Such grace, beauty, loveliness and life richly bestowed!
Dispense with Him, O misery and error.

Fly, O bird, fly to your natural home,
Your wings are outspread, your cage open.

Voyage from this bitter stream towards life's waters,
Return from the vestibule to the high seat of the soul.

Make haste, O soul! For we too are coming
From this world of duality to that of union.

How long shall we fill our laps with dust, stones
And such stuff from this world, like children?

Let us give up this world and fly towards Heaven,
Let us flee childhood to the banquet of men.

Behold, how your body has entrapped you!
Tear the sack and raise clear your head.

Take this scroll from Love with your right hand;
You are no child, not knowing right from left.

God said to Reason's messenger, 'Go',
To the hand of Death he said, 'World desire, chastise.'

A voice came to the spirit, 'Deliver me to the unseen'.
Take what gains, what treasure, and regret no more pain.

Cry out, announce that you are King;
In reply is your grace, in question your knowledge.

30

Of all the world I choose you alone;
Will you allow me to sit in grief?

My heart is as a pen in your hand;
You cause me to be either glad or sad.

Save what you will, what will have I?
Save what you reveal, what do I see?

Out of me you grow a thorn or a rose;
I smell roses now, and pull out thorns.

If you keep me as I am, I am;
If you change me, I'm changed.

In the glass where you colour my soul
I'm who? What is my Love or hate?

You were first, and last you shall be;
Make my last better than my first, do.

When you're hidden, I'm faithless;
When you're visible, I'm faithful.

I'm nothing, except what you've bestowed;
What do you seek from my breast and sleeve?

31

What can be done, O believers, as I don't recognize
  myself?
I'm neither a Christian nor Jew, Magian nor Moslem.

I'm not of the East or West, neither land nor sea;
I'm not of Nature's mine, nor the stars in Heaven.

I'm not of earth, water, air or fire;
I'm not of Heaven, nor the dust on this carpet.

I'm not of India, China, Bulgaria nor Saqsin;
I'm not of the kingdom of Iraq, nor Khorasan.

I'm not of this world, nor the next, Paradise nor Hell;
I'm not of Adam, nor Eve, Eden nor Rizwan.

My place is in the Placeless, my trace in the Traceless;
I'm neither body nor soul, as I belong to the soul of the
  Beloved.

I have dispensed with duality, and seen the two worlds as
  One;
One I seek, One I know, One I see, One I call.

He is the first, last, the outward and the inward,
I know none other than He, and He Who Is.

Love's cup intoxicated me as two worlds slip from my
  hands.
My only business now is carousing and revelry.

If once in my life I spent a moment without you,
From that moment on I repent my whole life.

If once in this world I win a moment with you,
Both worlds I'd trample under a dance of triumph.

O Shems of Tabriz, in this world I'm so drunk – now
Only stories of drunkenness and revelry pass my lips.

32

Apart from you my Beloved, I've found no joy in the two
worlds.
Though I've seen many wonders, none compare with you.

They say that a fire blazing is the unbeliever's lot:
I've seen none, except Abu Lahab, excluded from your
fire.

Many times I've laid the ear of the spirit near the heart's
window:
Long conversations I heard, yet those lips remained
invisible.

Suddenly you lavished grace upon your servant:
There was no reason for it but your infinite kindness.

O chosen cup-bearer, apple of my eye, your like
Have I never seen in Persia or Arabia.

Pour out wine until I become absent from myself;
In selfhood and existence I've felt only fatigue.

O you who are milk and sugar, sun and moon,
O you who are mother and father, no other kin have I
known.

O indestructible Love, O divine Minstrel,
You are both stay and refuge: no other name equals you.

We are but iron filings, your love the magnet:
You are source of all aspiration, myself I have seen none.

Silence, O Brother! Put learning and culture aside:
Until culture was named, I knew no culture but you.

33

I'm the beggar who pleads with you;
For me, the anguish inspired by your charms is
    inexhaustibly charming.

As the sun you blind me with the radiance of your beauty;
If I lower my gaze, who shall I look at?

Your harsh treatment will not cause me to betray you;
My constancy will restrain you from cruelty.

When I complained to you, you said, 'Provide your own
    remedy.'
My heart provides a remedy for Divine affliction.

If I spoke of it, my heart's grief would weary you;
I'll shorten this story, for mine is interminable grief.

34

As a painter I paint pictures, beauty I shape at every
   moment;
Yet in your presence I cause them to melt away.

A hundred phantoms I invoke and imbue them with
   spirits;
Behold, when I see your phantom I cast them into the fire.

Are you the winemaker's cup-bearer, or the enemy of a
   sober man,
Or is it you who ruins every house I build?

My soul dissolves in you, and with you is mingled;
Lo! My soul I cherish, because in it your fragrance lingers.

Every drop of blood flowing from me cries out to the
   earth:
'Your Love and I have blended, your affection and mine
   are partners.'

In this mud-brick house my heart is desolate without you;
O Beloved, enter this house, otherwise I'll leave.

35

To fly towards Heaven, this is Love,
Every instant, to tear a hundred veils.

The first moment is to renounce life;
To travel without feet the final step.

Look upon the world as invisible,
Doubt what is visible to oneself.

'O heart,' I said, 'may it bless you
To have entered the lover's circle,

'To look beyond the eye's range,
Penetrate the windings of the breast!

'O my soul, where did I receive this breath?
Where this pounding, O my heart?

'O bird, speak the language of the birds:
I alone understand your hidden meaning.'

Soul answered, 'I was in the divine kiln
When this water-and-clay house was baking.

'I quit this workshop of reality
While the building was under construction.

'No longer able to resist, they dragged me
Away, moulding me into the shape of a ball.'

36

O lovers, lovers, it's time to abandon the world;
From Heaven, the drum of departure pounds on my
    spirit's ear.

Behold, the driver has risen, made ready each line of camels,
Begging us not to blame him: why, O pilgrims, are you
    still asleep?

At front and behind there's din of departure and the
    sound of camel-bells;
At every moment a soul and spirit is setting off into the
    Void.

From the sky's blue awning and candle-lit stars
Have emerged people of wonder, mysteries revealed.

A deep sleep fell upon you from the orbiting planets:
Beware of the easy life, the unawakened doze!

O soul, find the Beloved, O friend, find the Friend,
O watchman, remain awake: it does no good for you to
    fall asleep.

On every side hubbub and chaos, in every street candles
    and torches,
Tonight the world teems, giving birth to a new and
    everlasting order.

Once dust you're now spirit, once ignorant now wise;
He who has led you so far will guide you further.

How pleasant are the pains he makes you suffer, while
    drawing you gently to himself!
His flames are like water: their wetness won't burn!

Inhabiting the soul is his task, breaking vows of penitence
also;
His artifice causes every atom to tremble at its core.

Stupid puppet, leaping on stage! As if to say 'I'm Lord of
the land.'
How high will you jump? Kneel, or they will bend you like
a bow.

You sowed the seed of deceit, and indulged in contempt,
You saw God as nothing. Look again, O wretch!

Ass, you fared better with straw; as a cauldron you were
better black;
You were best at the bottom of a well, O bringer of
disgrace to house and family!

In me there's Another who makes my eyes sparkle;
Know this, if water scalds it's my fire that makes it.

There's no stone in my hand, I'm at odds with no one,
I deal harshly with none, since I'm as sweet as a rose-
garden.

What I see derives its source from another universe;
Here and there a world: I sit on the threshold.

Those who sit there remain mute with silence;
It's enough to intimate this: hold your tongue, say no
more.

37

I've heard you intend travelling: don't.
Nor bestow your love on any new friend.

Though in this world you feel strange, know you've never
    been estranged;
Whatever pain you hope to wreak upon yourself: try not.

Don't steal away from me, or seek out foreigners;
Glancing stealthily at another is also useless.

O moon, for whose sake the heavens are confused,
You who offer me anguish and confusion; don't.

Where is the pledge, the compact you made with me?
You who wander from these so easily: beware!

Why make promises, and why protest,
Why make a shield of vows and gestures? Don't.

O you whose vestibule is above what is, and isn't,
At this moment you're fading from existence: don't.

O you who command Hell and Paradise to obey,
For me, you're making Paradise like Hell: don't.

I'm secure from blight in my field of cane;
Yet with sugar you mingle poison: don't.

Though my soul burns like a furnace, yet you're not
    happy;
My face pales gold at your absence: don't.

When you conceal your face, in grief the moon darkens;
Refrain from offering the moon an eclipse.

Our lips chap at the onset of your drought;
So why make my eyes tearful? Don't.

Since you dislike the intellectual rigour of lovers,
Why do you so dazzle reason's eye? Don't.

You deny delicacies to one sick of restraint;
Don't make your patient's health even worse.

My thieving eye steals your beauty;
O Beloved, don't punish my lawless sight.

Withdraw, friend, there's no time for flowery words;
Why intrude into the confusion of love? Don't.

If you decide to toss a glance in the two worlds' direction,
    then don't,
Except towards Shems' beauty, Wild One, and pride of
    Tabriz.

38

How happy we are when seated in a palace, you and I,
With dual forms and bodies but with one soul, you and I.

Birds' voices and the grove's moody colours offer
Immortality when we enter the garden, you and I.

Above, stars will emerge and gaze upon us;
We'll reveal to them the moon's splendour, you and I.

Individuals no more, you and I shall mingle in ecstasy
Full of joy, and beyond the reach of stupid talk.

All the hearts of Heaven's high-plumaged birds will be
    rotten with envy,
In the place where our laugh sounds similar, you and I.

The greatest wonder is this: that we sit here in the same
    spot,
In Iraq and Khorasan at this moment, you and I.

39

Visiting the Master's house, I said: 'Where is He?'
He replied, 'The Master is in love, dead drunk, a
    pilgrim.'

I said: 'I'm not obliged, but at least give me a clue;
He's my friend, nor am I his enemy.'

They replied: 'He's fallen in love with the Gardener;
Look for him among jasmine, or on the river-bank.'

Mad, crazy lovers always pursue what they love;
Yet all who fall in love – go, wash your hands of him!

Any fish that knows water refuses to land:
Should a lover languish among colour and perfume?

Snowdrifts that have witnessed the Sun's face
Are swallowed by the sun, though frozen in piles.

Especially one who's our King's lover,
Sweet-tempered and faithful, peerless being.

O infinite alchemy, which none can measure or doubt,
With one touch you make copper gold when 'Return' is
    uttered.

Sleep the world away, flee all six dimensions;
How long will you wander about, stupid and confused?

Inevitably they'll drag you, by your own consent,
Into the King's presence, where honours are
    bequeathed.

Had not an intruder been amongst us, Jesus
Might have revealed his mysteries, point by point.

I've chosen to mouth words, opening the secret way;
And in one moment I'm free from the desire to speak.

40

O my soul, who is this living in the heart's house?
Who occupies the throne save King and Prince?

With his hand he beckoned, saying, 'What do you desire
     from me?'
What does a drunk man desire most, but more wine and
     delicacies?

Delicacies drawn from the soul, Absolute Light in a cup,
One long banquet in the privacy of 'He as Truth.'

How many liars are there at the wine-bibbers' feast!
O facile man, take care you don't fall down!

Beware! Don't associate with criminals,
Your eyes shut like buds, your mouth open-rosed.

The world is like a mirror, your love the perfect image;
Lucky are they who have seen a whole greater than its
     parts.

Like grass walk on foot, because in this garden
The Beloved, rose-risen, rides before the hordes.

He is both sword and swordsman, the slain and slayer,
At once all Reason, he makes light of Reason.

That King is the Goldsmith, may he live forever,
May his loving hand remain a jewel about my neck!

41

I noticed my Beloved wandering about the house:
Taking up a fiddle, he played a tune.

His fingers were on fire as he played a song, still
Drunk and distraught after last night's revels.

He called up the cup-bearer in an Iraqi manner:
Wine was his real object, the cup-bearer his excuse.

Pitcher in hand, a comely cup-bearer
Stepped out of the shade to serve him.

The first cup he filled with sparkling wine –
Have you ever seen water put to the flame?

Those in love, for their sake he passed it around,
Then bowed, raised his head, and kissed the lintel.

My Beloved received a cup from him, and drank:
Across his face flame flashed in an instant.

Regarding his own beauty, he remarked to the evil-eye,
'In this age or the last there's never been one like me.

'I'm the Divine Sun of the world, the Beloved of lovers,
Soul and spirit are forever moving about me.'

42

Make yourself one of the Brotherhood, know their joy;
Enter the tavern quarter, observe the wine drinkers.

Drain passion's cup, and be not ashamed;
Close off the head's gaze, see instead the hidden eye.

Open your arms wide, wide! if you want to embrace;
Crush clay idols: behold, the face of the Fair!

For the sake of a crone, why live with so large a dowry?
For the sake of three loaves, why grab a sword and
    spear?

At night the Beloved always returns, so refrain from
    swooning on opium this eve.
Don't eat either, the mouth's sweetness is enough.

Remember, the cup-bearer is no tyrant, his assembly
    encircles:
Enter his orbit, and forget those cycles of time.

Take heed of this bargain: by giving up one life receive
    unnumbered.
Stop behaving as wolves or dogs do, know then the
    Shepherd's love.

You said, 'My enemy took all away from me':
Deny that person, contemplate His being instead.

Think of nothing but the creator of thought;
Know that caring for one's soul is better than bread.

When God's earth is so broad, why fall asleep in prison?
Avoid knotty problems, await your answers in Paradise.

Try not to speak, so you may weave words hereafter;
Give up life in this world, so you may know the Life of the
other.

43

Knowledge has recently arrived: perhaps you lack it.
All envious hearts bleed: perhaps you have none.

The moon's face unfolds, winged and radiant:
Borrow someone's soul whose eyes can see it!

From a hidden bow night and day arrow.
This life yield up since you have no shield.

Like Moses, has not your verdigris of a life been made gold
  by his alchemy?
Though you've no sack full of gold, there's the Koran.

Within you is sweet Egypt, for you are a field of sugar;
Does it matter you're not supplied from without?

A slave to form, you worship craven images;
Resembling Joseph, yet you fail to reflect on yourself.

By God! When you see your own beauty mirrored
You'll become your own idol, and not look at anyone.

O Reason, comparing him to the moon: is it wrong?
By doing so, perhaps your vision has failed you.

Your head is but a lamp with six wicks:
Without that spark, would any remain alight?

Your camel of a body tramps to the soul's Ka'aba;
Your *Haj* failed because your nature is an ass, not that you
  have no mount.

If you haven't yet reached the Ka'aba, luck will lead you
  there.
Don't hide, O babbler, from God there's no refuge.

44

O Heart, why are you a prisoner of this passing earth?
Fly from this cage, like a bird of a more winged world.

As a beloved friend, hiding behind a veil, why
Do you make this realm of transience your home?

Take stock of yourself, then make your escape
From this formal world's prison, into a field of ideas.

You're a bird of the Holy Land, a friend at the court of
    Love;
To remain here too long is not advised.

Every morning a voice calls to you from Heaven:
'Shed the dust of the journey, and the goal is yours.'

You'll find in every thorn-bush on the road to the Ka'aba
    of union
Thousands dead from desire, whose lives were
    courageously given.

Many more fell wounded on this path, deprived of
Union's fragrance – that Friend's sweet perfume.

In memory of union's feast, and longing for his beauty
Many have fallen down drunk on common wine.

In the hope of seeing him, what a joy it is to stand in his
    doorway!
To look upon his face is enough to turn night into day!

Throw light on the body's senses with the light of the soul:
Each sense has its prayer, the heart two more.

The sun, moon, and axis of the seven heavens are
   consumed
By the Canopus of the soul, rising in the south.

Don't look for fame and fortune in this world, they're not
   to be found;
Look for happiness through Him in both worlds.

Forget the story of love that travellers tell;
Serve God with all your strength instead.

From the Sun, glory of Tabriz, seek future happiness.
As the Sun shines, His knowledge is enthroned.

45

Be mindful, you'll not know a friend like me.
Where in the world is there such a Beloved?

Be mindful, don't spend your life wandering about,
There's no market elsewhere for you to splurge.

You are as an arid gully, I as rain,
You are a city in ruins, I the architect.

Know that my service is like joy at dawn,
Few men experience its illuminating warmth.

In dreams you see a myriad shifting images;
When the dream ends you're left with nought.

Close tight the eye of falsity, open wide the eye of the
    intellect;
An ass is your senses, evil thoughts its halter.

Choose sweet syrup from the garden of Love, for Nature
Sells vinegar, and crushes unripened grapes.

Enter the hospital of your Creator, for no man
Who's ill can dispense with his remedies.

Without the King the world is decapitated:
Like a turban, fold yourself about its severed head.

Unless you're dark, don't let the mirror fall
From your hand: soul is your mirror, your body rust.

Where is the lucky merchant, whose destiny Jupiter
Controls, that I may trade with him and buy his wares?

Come, remember me who gave you the ability to think,
From my mine you may yet buy an ass-load of rubies.

Come, walk towards him who gave you feet,
Look with both eyes on him who gave you sight.

Clap hands for joy of him, by whose foamy hand
The sea is made. His joy dispels sorrow and pain.

Speak without tongue, without ears listen,
The tongue's mutterings often give offence.

46

Upon Love's face gaze, that you may be considered a man.
Don't sit with cold people; their breath will chill you.

Seek from Love's face something other than beauty;
It's time you associated with a genuine friend.

A clod of earth, you'll not rise in the air
Unless you break and become mere dust.

If you don't break, he who made you will;
When death does, will you remain separate?

A fresh root makes green again a leaf that yellows;
So don't blame Love at your increasing paleness.

O friend, if you attain perfection among us,
This throne will be yours, your every desire gained.

But if you remain too long on this earth,
You will be as dice, passing from place to place.

If Shems of Tabriz, O Wild One! draws you to his side,
On your escape from gaol, you'll re-enter his orbit.

47

When I entered your city, you chose a separate corner;
When I left, you failed to look or bid me goodbye.

Whether you choose to be filled with spite or kindly,
All of you is the soul's comfort, the feast's adornment.

The cause of your jealousy is your hiddenness,
Your every atom is concealed, like the sun in cloud.

If you live alone, aren't you the Prince's darling?
And if you tear down the veil, all veils are torn.

You confuse an untrue heart, your wine makes drunk a
    faithful mind;
Drawing all towards you, all sense is outlawed.

All roses wither in winter, all heads slump on wine:
Yet from the hand of death you recover these blooms.

Since no rose is constant, why worship every bloom?
You alone are reliable, our one stay and support.

If a few wound themselves for the sake of Joseph,
You deprive a myriad Josephs of soul and reason.

Man's form you mould foul or fair, so he
May run a mile from the stench of decay.

A speck of dust you make of him, that he may become
    sweet grass;
From filth he is free when your soul's breath is inhaled.

O heart, fly towards Heaven, eat pure pasture,
You've grazed long enough among cattle.

Fix your whole desire on what seems hopeless,
You've come a long way from that first failure.

Be silent so that the Lord of Language may speak,
He fashioned the door and lock, also the key.

48

At last you've left and gone to the Invisible;
How marvellous the way you quit this world.

You ruffled your feathers and, breaking free of your
    cage,
You took to the air, bound for the soul's world.

A favoured falcon, you were caged by an old woman:
When the falcon-drum sounded, you flew into the Void.

A love-sick nightingale among owls, you caught
The scent of roses, and flew to the rose-garden.

From this bitter brew you suffered a hangover;
At last you set out for Eternity's tavern.

Like an arrow you sped for the mark;
From this bow bliss was your target.

Like a thorn the world nettled you with false clues;
Dismissing them, you plucked that which is clueless.

Since you're now the Sun, why wear a crown?
Why wear a belt when you're gone at the waist?

I hear you look at your soul with dim eyes:
Why gaze at it at all, you're already en-Souled?

O heart, what a flighty bird you are. In the chase for divine
    reward
Your two wings flew to the point of a spear like a shield!

From autumn roses run – what a fearless rose you are!
Wandering about in the company of a cold wind.

Falling as rain does on the roof of this world
You flowed all ways, then escaped down a drain.

Be silent, and free from the pain of speech; yet
Don't sleep now that you've found solace with a Friend.

49

In each Heaven I've circled with the nine Fathers,
For years I've convolved with the stars in their signs.

For a while I was invisible, then united with Him,
In the realm of 'or nearer' I witnessed all.

God gives me my food, like a child in the womb;
Man is born once, I many times.

Wearing the cloak of my body, I worked hard in this
     world,
I've often had to rip this cloak with my bare hands.

I've slept nights with monks in their monasteries,
I've slept with unbelievers before their idols.

I'm the booty of robbers, the pain of the sick;
Both cloud and rain, I've inundated fields.

O dervish! Never has annihilation's dust settled on my
     clothes.
I've gathered armfuls of roses from eternity's garden.

I'm neither fire nor water, nor the following wind;
I'm not clay either: since I've left them all behind.

O Son, I'm not Shems of Tabriz, but pure Light;
If you see me, look out! Tell no man either.

Bibliography

Al-Ghazzali *The Niche for Lights*, translated by W Gairdner, Royal Asiatic Society, London, 1924

Arberry, A J *Discourses of Rumi*, John Murray, London, 1961

Barks, Colman and Moyne, John *Open Secret, Versions of Rumi*, Threshold Books, USA, 1984

Defoe, Daniel *Robinson Crusoe*, Oxford University Press, Oxford, 1986

Corbin, Henry *Avicenna and the Visionary Recital*, Spring Publications, Octopus, London 1980

Ficino, Marcelio *Letters*, translated by Shepherd-Walwyn, 1975

Fischer-Dieskau, D. *Wagner and Nietzsche*, Seabury Press, New York, 1976

Helminski, Edmund *The Ruins of the Heart, Selected Lyric Poetry of Jaláluddin Rumi*, Threshold Books, USA, 1981

Iqbal, Afzal *The Life and Works of Jaláluddin Rumi*, The Octagon Press, London, 1983

Ibn Arabi, Muhiyddin *Kernel of the Kernel*, Beshara Publications, UK

Joyce, James *Ulysses*, Bodley Head, London, 1964

Kazantzakis, Nikos *Zorba the Greek*, Faber Books, London, 1961

Lewis, Bernard *The Assassins*, Weidenfeld and Nicolson, London, 1967

Lings, Martin *What is Sufism?* Mandala Books, London, 1975

Miller, Arthur *The Time of the Assassins*, New Directions, USA, 1962

Mohammed *The Koran*, translated by A.J. Arberry, Oxford University Press, Oxford, 1982

Nicholson, R.A. *Rumi, Poet and Mystic*, George Allen and Unwin, London, 1956

——*Divani Shamsi Tabriz*, Cambridge University Press, Cambridge, 1898

Nietzsche, Friedrich *Beyond Good and Evil*, Allen and Unwin, London, 1967
—— *The Case Against Wagner*, Fisher Unwin, London, 1899
Onder, Mehmet *Mevlana and the Whirling Dervishes*, Guven Matbaasi, Ankara, 1977
Ozturk, Yasar Nuri *The Eye of the Heart, An Introduction to Sufism*, Redhouse Press, Istanbul, 1988
Roditi, Elouard *Yunus Emre: The Wandering Fool, Sufi Poems of a Thirteenth-century Turkish Dervish*, Cadmus Editions, USA, 1987
Roskill, Mark *The Letters of Van Gogh*, Fontana Classics, New York, 1972
Schimmel, Annemarie *The Triumphal Sun, A Study of the Works of Jaláluddin Rumi*, East-West Publications, London and The Hague, 1980
—— *As Through a Veil, Mystical Poetry in Islam*, Columbia University Press, New York, 1982
Schuon, Frithjof *Understanding Islam*, Penguin Paperbacks, London, 1972
Starkie, Enid *Arthur Rimbaud*, Faber Books, London, 1973
Suhrawardi, Shihabuddin *The Mystical and Visionary Treatises*, Octagon Press, London, 1982